OVERHEAD

OVERHEAD

What It Is and How It Works

JACK F. FULTZ

Abt Books | Cambridge
Massachusetts

Printed in the United States of America

Library of Congress Cataloging in Publication Data

Fultz, Jack F   1932-
  Overhead, what it is and how it works.

  Includes index.
  1. Overhead costs—Accounting. 2. Cost accounting.
I. Title.
HF5681.08F84   657'.42   79-57519
ISBN 0-89011-547-9

HF5681
.08 F 84

Contents

Preface

A few years ago I was on an assignment in Costa Rica. My role was to design and implement a cost control system for a major transportation project. While visiting Costa Rica, I had the opportunity to spend a weekend at a black volcanic ash beach with a fellow American engineer and two project engineers from Columbia, South America. While relaxing in the bright tropic sun, I noticed a thatched roof spread across four poles and a Pepsi Cola sign hanging from one of the poles. Since it was very warm, I volunteered to buy the Pepsi if we all walked to the booth. One of the Spanish speaking engineers ordered the four Pepsis. The proprietor charged an amount about equivalent to one dollar in U.S. currency. This surprised me because one of my most vivid impressions of Costa Rica was how inexpensive it was to eat a full meal in any restaurant. I realized the dollar I paid for the four Pepsis was almost three times what I paid for lunches at the transportation department's cafeteria. I made an off-hand comment to no one in particular that the Pepsis were expensive. This started a five-minute conversation in Spanish between one of the Columbian engineers and the proprietor. When they had finished the conversation the engineer came over to us smiling. I asked what the conversation was about. He said the proprietor had heard my remark and was explaining about the high cost of overhead. Now I don't know what heavy costs were associated with four wooden poles, a thatched roof, bottles of Pepsi, and a couple of tubs of ice, but I began to appreciate that the word overhead has a great many meanings to different people.

The purpose of this book is to provide the reader with an overall working knowledge of overhead — what it is, how it is used, and how it is calculated. The basic book is followed by five appendices. Appendix A is provided as a self-review of the material contained in the main part of the book. Appendix B provides several worksheets that outline step-by-step procedures for calculating indirect cost rates. Appendix C is a detailed review of the items of allowable and unallowable costs included in the Federal Procurement Regulations Cost Principles. Appendix D explains the difference between expense by type and expense by purpose and presents definitions for the most commonly used expense classification. The assumption has been made that the reader has an understanding or a reasonable familiarity with the basic concepts of the accounting equation and the use of debits and credits. However, for review purposes, a brief explanation of these concepts is included in Appendix E.

The book has been written at a level that will permit the non-accountant to read and understand the principle of overhead. The busy executive can read selected portions in order to grasp the overall concept without getting involved in details. This person should carefully read Chapters 1 through 4. For the person who wants to understand the full concept and how it works in practice, it is recommended that the entire book be read. While a review of the appendices would be helpful, it should not be necessary to study these in detail. For the student or the office worker who wants to understand the concept in detail, the entire book should be read and studied, including careful attention to the appendices. The book is designed to teach specific day-to-day accounting concepts at a practical level. After reading the book and completing the exercises in Appendix A, the reader should be able to understand the underlying concept and use the practical information gleaned from the book to assist in making the transition from theory to practice.

1

Definition of Terms

There is an almost endless array of problems associated with rising material and labor costs and an equal amount of offsetting potential solutions. So, when a firm experiences a drop in operating profit not connected with a corresponding reduction in revenue, management can readily determine which element of the sales dollar has increased in cost. If material cost has increased because of a rise in the cost of the components of the products, some possible courses of action include substituting a less expensive material, mass buying to obtain lower per-unit costs, or reviewing the latest technology to see if an alternative component mix would produce a lower per-unit cost.

If the rise in cost occurs in the area of production labor, some possible solutions include changing the mix of the labor by using less expensive staff than was previously used, finding more cost-effective ways to fabricate the product, or getting more productivity from the present staff. Of course, if the cost increase cannot be reduced through technical or financial innovative methods, management may be forced to increase the price of the product.

The point is that a rise in material and labor costs is easily recognized by management and can be anticipated and dealt with directly. However, if the reduction in profit is occasioned by an increase in non-product costs, the solutions are not always as evident because the particular cause of the increase may not be detectable without a detailed analysis. The nature of overhead, or non-product related costs, is such that the expenses are spread across a number of accounts of various types of expenditures occurring differentially over a period of time. Therefore, the rise in overhead expenses occurs more slowly, may be less noticeable, requires more internal control, and results from a multitude of simultaneous and dissimilar actions of management. Management must be constantly aware of, and understand the composition of, these overhead costs in order to be able to control them effectively.

Although the term overhead is common in industry, there are a number of other terms that are and can be used interchangeably. Some of these terms are indirect expenses, burden, expense pool, manufacturing or engineering expense, overhead expense, indirect cost, factory or plant expense, loading, and support costs. Before a detailed discussion of overhead is undertaken, it is important to define a number of terms that will appear throughout this work. This chapter will attempt to provide the reader with an understanding of the term cost objective, to clarify the difference between direct and indirect charges, and to present an overview of the elements of cost.

COST OBJECTIVE

A *cost objective* is any function for which cost is accumulated. The decision to establish cost objectives is made by management based on its need for summarized cost information. However, decisions about establishing cost objectives are greatly influenced by the cost and time required to obtain this cost information.

Cost objectives are classified according to management's use of the information. Two broad classifications are *output cost objectives* and *organizational cost objectives*. Examples of output cost objectives are products, client contracts, and other management projects, whether covered by a signed contract or not. Examples of organizational cost objectives are plants, offices, departments, branches, or cost centers.* Stated simply, a cost objective is any accumulation of cost defined by management in order to meet its information needs for operational decision making.

DIRECT AND INDIRECT CHARGES

A *direct charge* is one that is incurred for a specific cost objective. The charges must be positively related to that cost objective, and the cost objective must receive specific benefit for the cost incurred. The type of the expense does not determine whether it is direct or indirect. The same type of expense may be treated as a direct expense in one company and as an indirect expense in another company; it may also have both characteristics within the same company.

By definition, then, all expenses are direct expenses of the business as a whole. If a business is organized by departments, then expenses that are direct to the business as a whole may be indirect to the departments. Real estate taxes, for example, would be a direct charge to the total business but would be an indirect expense to the department. But if the tax expense could be segregated and associated with the department, then the expense would be direct to the department as well. The concept of direct and indirect charges can be understood by a review of the following illustrations.

The cost of telephones can be charged as direct and/or indirect. If the expense can be associated with specific cost objectives, then it is charged as direct; otherwise, it is charged as indirect. In some organizations, telephone calls are monitored and are charged directly to specific cost objectives, but the equipment, advertisement, and tax portion of the expense is treated as an indirect expense.

Supplies can also be charged as direct and/or indirect. Many companies will treat all supplies as indirect expenses on the theory that it costs too much to control the expenses or that the record-keeping costs are too high for the benefit received. Other firms treat supplies as a direct expense by maintaining a perpetual inventory and costing each issuance of supplies at the actual cost. This is

---

*The examples should make it clear that output cost objectives relate to cost accumulated for specific projects or assignments, whereas organizational cost objectives relate to functional breakdowns of the organization.

done by charging the cost objectives with the average cost or by allocating the supplies to the cost objective on some other equitable basis. All of these methods require that a physical inventory be taken at the end of the year with the variance from actual supplies on hand charged to profit or loss. It is important to note that charging an expense as direct does not mean that the actual unit cost must be known. An expense can be charged on an estimated basis if the method used results in a logical and equitable cost distribution. The method of treating all supplies as direct expenses, or as an indirect one, is used, but most firms use a combination of both ways.

It is the responsibility of the accounting management to review expenses. Those that have a high cost relative to other expenses and are easy to segregate for cost purposes are treated as direct; the balance of expenses are treated as indirect.

In summary, if the cost is identifiable and benefits a specific cost objective, then it is charged directly to that cost objective. If the expense cannot be identified with, or does not benefit, a particular cost objective, it is charged to overhead and redistributed or reallocated to those cost objectives that do benefit from it.

ELEMENTS OF COST

Exhibit 1, "Analysis of Selling Price," illustrates a typical manufacturing firm's cost breakdown. A manufacturing firm was chosen for this discussion of elements of cost because it generally incorporates all types of costs [i.e., prime or direct charges and the major types of overhead — plant overhead (manufacturing, engineering), selling, and general and administrative costs].

Traditionally, a nongovernment organization's cost is divided into two major parts — the production portion and the commercial portion. The production portion includes the material used to build the product, the engineering labor used to design and develop it, the manufacturing labor used on the materials that form the product, and all accompanying overhead. The commercial portion consists of the distribution, selling, and administrative expenses.

A review of Exhibit 1 reveals that the material costs, production (direct) labor, and other direct charges are referred to as prime costs or direct costs. As stated earlier, direct costs are those incurred for a

Exhibit 1

Analysis of Selling Price

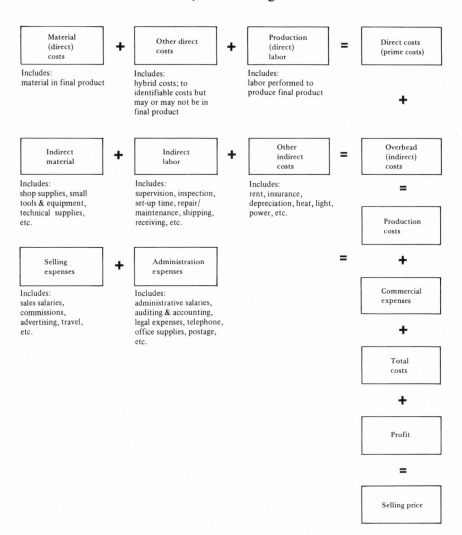

specific cost objective. And so, direct material refers to all material that forms an integral part of the finished product and that can be included in calculating the cost of that product.

The ease with which material can be traced to the final product has a great deal to do with whether the material is considered as a direct material. For example, glue and tacks to build furniture and electronic components (such as diodes, capacitors, etc.) used in missiles are all undoubtedly part of finished products, but for costing purposes they are rarely classified as direct materials. They are generally considered too small and too inexpensive to justify either the cost or the time required to keep track of their cost. For convenience they are usually grouped as an overhead expense or are allocated to specific cost objectives as "other direct charges," and an allocation formula that provides an equitable distribution of costs is used to calculate the expense.

Direct labor is the labor expended on the material to convert it into the finished product. It usually consists of the wages allocable to a particular product and traceable to that product and is referred to as productive labor.

Although direct labor is subject to some difference in actual practice, it generally possesses two characteristics: it is directly attributed to a product or service and it is an amount sufficient to merit identification and measurement.

Some labor, such as inspection labor, falls into a broader category where it can be treated either as direct or indirect labor. Differences in treatment are found both among individual firms within industries and among various industries.

It should also be noted that direct labor refers only to straight time payments to employees and does not include the premium portion of overtime pay. For example, if Mr. Jones earns $5.00 per hour and works 2 hours of overtime for which he was paid time-and-one-half, he would earn $15.00 for the 2 hours [2 hours x 7.50 (5.00 x 1½) = $15.00]. The direct labor portion of the $15.00 would be $10.00 (2 hours x $5.00 per hour straight time). The premium portion would be $5.00 [2 hours x 2.50 (½ of the hourly rate)] and would not be considered direct labor. It would be classified as a nonlabor charge and called other direct charges.

OTHER DIRECT CHARGES

A special class of costs, referred to as other direct charges (ODC), has developed and has all of the properties of a direct material cost, yet may or may not be a tangible part of the final product. Direct costs was defined earlier as a cost that can be consistently and economically measured to one or more cost objective that receives the benefit of that cost. Although not generally considered a major component of the product, ODC nevertheless benefits a particular cost objective, can be measured, and the amount of the cost is significant enough to warrant its tracking. A look at three examples may help to clarify this hybrid classification.

If one considers the manufacture of an easy chair, it is clear that both the labor to fabricate the frame and the labor to cover the frame with fabric are direct costs (direct labor). Likewise, the wood in the frame and the material to cover the frame are direct costs (material). But what about the glue, tacks, and staples used in the construction? These materials are used in the final product and could be charged to the product as an other direct charge (ODC)— *if* it were easy to measure their cost to the particular product or their cost could be included in overhead. It is a decision that each company makes depending upon its overhead structure.

If a systems analyst were retained as a consultant to provide corporate management assistance on several diverse but general projects, the cost would be considered an indirect cost and included, in overhead. However, if the time the consultant spent benefitted and was measurable to particular cost objectives, then the cost would be charged to each particular cost objective on which the consultant worked and would be classified as other direct charges (ODC).

If a lawyer provides general service to corporate management, then this expense would be charged to overhead. However, if that lawyer provides service on a subject directly related to a particular cost objective and the time and cost connected with this work could be measured, then the cost could be charged as an other direct cost (ODC).

Exhibit 2 illustrates typical expenses that are charged in this cost classification. A review of this exhibit shows that these expenses can be charged either as direct or indirect, depending upon the accounting structure used and the benefit received. The classification of other direct charges (ODC) is a hybrid that will vary from company to company.

Several minor expenses are frequently charged as indirect expenses because of the cost and difficulty associated with keeping records of these costs. A general rule to be followed is that *if the cost of more precise measurement is greater than the benefit received, the cost should be treated as an indirect or overhead expense.*

Exhibit 2

Typical Other Direct Charges Items

Travel
Telephone
Reproduction
Postage
Computer Costs
Subcontract Service
Consultant
Graphics
Premium on Overtime Worked

2

What are Overhead Costs?

Both the Federal Procurement regulations and the Armed Service Procurement regulations provide the following definition of overhead:

> "An indirect or overhead cost is one which because of its incurrence for common or joint objectives is not readily subject to treatment as a direct cost. Minor direct cost items may be considered to be indirect costs for reasons of practicality. After direct costs have been determined and directly charged to contracts or other work as appropriate, indirect costs are those remaining to be allocated to several classes."

This work defines overhead as: (1) those expenses incurred for the *common good* of several cost objectives and which cannot be reasonably or cost-effectively charged directly to specific cost objectives; (2) those expenses that could be allocated logically to specific cost objectives except that the benefit received is not in consonance with the cost distributed; (3) those expenses that are so minor as to make it impractical for both cost and time reasons to charge them directly to a particular cost objective.

These costs are simply added together to form a "pool" of costs known as overhead. They are distributed to those cost objectives that received benefits in a rational and logical manner.

DISTINGUISHING AMONG TYPES OF OVERHEAD

Overhead or indirect expenses are segregated into three basic categories — regular company overhead, selling expense, and general and administrative expense. The following sections provide a brief overview of the types of expenses included in each category and illustrate how the expenses are accounted for in a commercial firm.

COMPANY OVERHEAD

Company overhead represents those costs not directly attributable to a particular product or service that are incurred either in support of a product's production or in support of offering a service. Illustrative examples of overhead expenses are shop or operating supervisory support; general repair and maintenance of the plant or office; power, heat, and light; and freight or cartage expense. (A more detailed breakdown will be supplied later.) The basis for allocating these costs quite obviously varies from organization to organization, but in all cases the basis is chosen so that the costs are equitably distributed to the products or services in relation to the benefits received. Examples of bases (also discussed in detail later) are machine hours, direct cost, direct labor hours, and direct labor dollars.

SELLING EXPENSE

Selling expense represents the costs associated with the physical distribution of the product or service, as well as advertising and related marketing expenses, including sales department support personnel. In addition to advertising and distribution costs (packaging and shipping), public relations expenses and marketers' commissions or salaries are also common to this classification. In many large firms, the corporate expense for marketing management (direction and coordination of selling programs and strategies) are accumulated and then allocated to divisions, departments, or products on an equitable basis. The basis may be the sales of the division or product, the cost of the product or services being sold, or any basis chosen by management that is considered equitable and which is generally agreed upon by the corporate office and the division or product manager receiving the allocation. It is important to recognize that the distribution of the total corporate marketing expense is not an exact science but an allocation based upon the best estimate at the time.

GENERAL AND ADMINISTRATIVE (G & A) EXPENSE

General and administrative expenses refers to those expenses necessary for the general overall operation of the business. Examples of costs associated with this category are general management costs, salaries of administrative and office staff who are not directly working for marketing or operating departments, office supplies, and corporate legal and auditing expenses. These costs are allocated on the basis of the cost of goods sold or total cost input — the total cost incurred in a fiscal year exclusive of the general administrative expense. The Cost Accounting Standards Board has excluded cost of sales as an acceptable basis. Therefore, effective for fiscal years starting after January 1, 1977, the only acceptable basis for allocation of costs on government contracts will be total cost input.

AN ILLUSTRATIVE DIFFERENCE

Is the difference among these three overhead pools just that they have different allocation bases, chosen according to the nature of the expense? No! There is one other major difference. Company overhead consists of costs associated with the product or service and it can be capitalized (included) in the cost of the product or service. Selling and general and administrative costs are considered period expenses related to a particular accounting period, and these cannot be capitalized or included in an inventory but must be written off against profit in the accounting period in which they are incurred. These costs are considered to be period costs; that is, expenses of the accounting period that should not be attached to the product or services. Obviously, selling expenses cannot be attached to inventories because they are not considered applicable to the product until the product is sold; and at that point, the product is no longer inventory. Some administrative expenses are incurred for purchasing and production warehousing and, theoretically, should be assigned to a product rather than be classified as a period cost. But as accounting principles developed, there appeared to be a traceable relationship between these indirect overhead expenses and the product. However, that relationship was so remote that a decision was made to charge off the expenses immediately under the normal accounting approach of conservatism.

For clarification purposes, assume that the Rayco Company manufactures radio cabinets. The first year of operation provides the following information:

Material	$20,000
Direct manufacturing labor	$15,000
Manufacturing overhead	$15,000
Selling expense	$20,000
Administrative expenses	$10,000
Revenue	$49,000
Selling price per cabinet	$ 7
Ending inventory (of cabinets)	3,000
Total cabinets produced	10,000

The $15,000 of direct labor (the labor used to produce cabinets) utilized $20,000 of material to produce the 10,000 cabinets during the year. The total cost of producing 10,000 cabinets was $50,000 (the sum of the $20,000 materials cost, the $15,000 direct labor, and the $15,000 company overhead). What is significant is that the company overhead can be capitalized in the cost of the cabinets. This means that the inventory cost per box was $5.00 ($50,000 total cost ÷ the 10,000 cabinets produced). Since the selling price is $7.00 per cabinet, Rayco must have sold 7,000 cabinets ($49.000 revenue ÷ $7.00 selling price = 7,000 cabinets sold). The cost of goods sold must have been $35,000 (7,000 units sold x $5.00 per unit). This is in agreement with the overall remaining inventory information shown below.

Total Inventory Cost Available	$50,000 (10,000 x $5.00)
Less Cost of Goods Sold	−35,000 (7,000 x $5.00)
Ending Inventory	$15,000 (3,000 x $5.00)

Since the selling and general administrative costs are period costs that are not included in inventory and must be written off in the accounting period incurred, the Rayco profit-and-loss statement for the first year looks like this:

Revenue	$49,000
Cost of Goods Sold	−35,000
Gross Profit	$14,000
Less: Selling Cost	20,000
G&A Costs	10,000
Loss on operations of the year	($16,000)

This illustration emphasizes the point made above, that company overhead is part of the product cost and can be included in inventory cost, whereas selling and general and administrative costs must be written off in the accounting period in which they are incurred.

If the selling and general administrative expense could have been included in inventory, quite a different profit and loss and inventory picture would have resulted, similar to the following:

Cost of Cabinets

Material	$20,000
Labor	15,000
Overhead	15,000
Selling	20,000
G&A	10,000
Total Cost of Cabinets	$80,000
Number of cabinets produced	10,000
Cost per cabinet	$ 8
Total revenue (7,000 x $7.00)	$49,000
Cost of goods sold (7,000 x $8.00)	56,000
Profit (Loss)	($ 7,000)

Total Inventory Cost Available	$80,000	(10,000 x $8.00)
Less Cost of Goods Sold	−56,000	(7,000 x $8.00)
Ending Inventory	$24,000	(3,000 x $8.00)

As shown below, if one includes selling and general and administrative expense in inventory, then $9,000 of the year's loss would be deferred from cost and included in inventory.

Ending Inventory (without selling and G & A expense)	$15,000
Ending Inventory (including selling and G & A expense)	24,000
Selling and G&A expense included in inventory	($ 9,000)

3

The Classification
of Overhead

Overhead has been defined as a summary of expenses that benefit more than one cost objective. Each firm develops its own system for classifying, recording, and summarizing overhead expenses. Regardless of the system used, all costs are usually accumulated in a book or in a set of ledgers called the general ledger. For simplifying rate calculations, the general ledger normally contains three summary accounts that accumulate the indirect expenses of overhead, selling, and general and administrative. However, if all individual indirect expenses incurred in a year were charged to only three large accounts, management would not be able to evaluate the cost of operations or to determine the cause of higher-than-anticipated indirect costs without extensive analysis. Such analysis would be both costly and time-consuming. Therefore, supporting these general ledger accounts are subsidiary ledger accounts.

THE GROUPING OF EXPENSES

The subsidiary ledger sheets are simply summaries of individual expenses grouped by like expenses. The grouping of these similar expenses together in logical subsets permits better expense control by management and facilitates cost analysis.

The subsidiary ledger can take one of several forms: individual sheets that immediately follow the control sheet in the general ledgers, a separate book, or a printout from the data processing section. In very small firms with a limited number of expenses, the general ledger sheets themselves may suffice, in which case there is no summary account.

The assignment of expenses to indirect cost pools as illustrated in this chapter is representative of standard practices in industry, but it should be recognized that there are many variations. Based on its needs for information, each corporate management group must make these decisions for itself, but the charging and the assignment of expenses and their allocation must be consistent from year to year. To assist in understanding the type of cost charged to each expense account, a brief definition is included in Appendix B to this work.

There is no one right way to group these expenses; the decision is dictated by management needs. However, a typical breakdown is the following:

  Indirect labor
  Allowed time
  Labor additives, benefits, or surcharges
  Supplies and indirect materials
  Professional and outside services
  Utilities and transportation
  Advertising, publicity, and promotion
  Travel, luncheons, and business meetings
  Employment, recruitment, and employee welfare
  Occupancy expenses
  Sundry group

No attempt has been made thus far to relate particular expenses to the three types of overhead controls. By collecting the cost of individual expenses in logical categories, management is able to monitor easily the costs of similar types of expenses. Individual expenses are reviewed only in the event that they appear unreasonable or out of line with what was anticipated.

The simplest form of cost system is one in which all of the overhead expenses are accumulated in one account and the total of these expenses is allocated to cost objectives on some common base. The common base must be chosen so that each cost objective receives an equitable share of the overhead expenses. The direct costs, labor, and material are added to the allocated overhead to obtain the total cost of the cost objective.

For illustrative purposes, if it is assumed that the total overhead expense is $125,000 and the base chosen is direct labor, which totaled $100,000, then the overhead rate would be 125 percent, calculated by the following formula:

$$\frac{\text{Total overhead}}{\text{Total direct labor}} = \frac{\$125,000}{\$100,000} = 125\%$$

If a particular cost objective used $100 of material and required $200 of direct labor, then the overhead rate of 125 percent would be applied to the direct labor to absorb its share of the overhead of $250 (200 x 125%), and a total cost would result as follows:

Materials	$100
Direct labor	200
Overhead @ 125% of direct labor costs	250
Total cost	$550

The previous illustration of expense categories ignores the difference in types of indirect expenses (i.e., company overhead, selling, and general and administrative). To help understand how individual expenses are separated into the major types of indirect expenses, a detailed breakdown of the typical grouping of expenses is presented below. Some expenses can be classified in more than one indirect expense pool.

This breakdown provides a representative array of the types of labor charged by individuals. Each industry and even each company will vary in its use of these classifications. While the cost of the executive classification is usually accumulated under the general and administrative category, the cost can be individually collected as a part of overhead selling, and general and administrative if the firm decides that it wants to record the cost of the operating, management, and selling executives in their respective indirect expense pools. Many firms do not record the individual labor cost to the details as outlined but record all the labor cost for these functions to two accounts— supervisory, and administrative and clerical. The extensive break- down presented below serves to illustrate the amount of flexibility possible.

	Indirect Expense Type		
Expense Classification	*Overhead*	*Selling*	*G&A*
Indirect Labor			
Executive			X
Supervisory	X	X	X
Administrative & clerical	X	X	X
Bidding & estimating proposal preparation		X	
Inspection	X		
General engineering	X		
Repair & maintenance building	X		
Repair & maintenance machinery & equipment	X		
Moving & rearranging	X		
Instrumentation & calibration	X		
Operating services — shipping & receiving	X		
Operating services — stores	X		
Operating services — production control	X		
Janitorial	X		X
Accounting			X
Contract services			X
Personnel services	X		X
Library services			X
Administrative services			X
Corporate planning			X
Corporate control			X
Policy formulation			X

The following illustration would be typical of the operation of a manufacturing facility. Many service industry firms prefer not to record the actual cost of nonproductive labor as an identifiable expense and instead bury it in general administrative costs. The words "nonproductive labor" are not meant to imply that the labor was not productive but rather that it was not direct to a specific cost objective.

Allowed & Idle Time	O/H	Selling	G&A
Waiting for material	X		
Waiting for set up	X		
Waiting for inspection	X		
Mechanical failure	X		
Electrical failure	X		

All of the expenses below are classified as employee fringe benefits. They can be accumulated in a separate control account and allocated to the other three overhead classifications. The trend in recent years, however, has been to associate the expense directly with the labor at the time the charge is being made. Some companies treat this cost as an additive to the labor charged, while others build the cost directly into the labor rate itself. Either method is acceptable. If the rate is used as an additive, it is important to know the actual cost at year's end so it can be allocated to the proper cost objective. If it is built into the labor rate, any variance from the estimate is recorded as an adjustment to each of the three overhead classifications in proportion to the actual labor charged during the year.

Labor Surcharges	Fringe Benefit
FICA payroll taxes (employer's share)	X
Unemployment payroll taxes (federal & state)	X
Workers' compensation	X
Group insurance	X
Holiday	X
Vacation	X
Sick leave	X
Profit sharing	X
Pension fund	X

The breakdown of supplies indicates that office supplies are charged to all three overhead classifications. Many firms prefer to charge all of this type of expense to general and administrative, while others prefer to associate their cost with the indirect expense pool that uses them. The decision is determined by the individual firm after considering the amount of the expense, the cost of distributing the expense, and the benefit received from making the distribution.

Supplies & Indirect Material	*O/H*	*Selling*	*G&A*
Office supplies	X	X	X
Small tools & equipment	X		
Repair & maintenance supplies	X		
Janitorial supplies	X		
Operating supplies	X		
Library & technical supplies			X
Printing & reproduction supplies	X	X	X

Professional and outside service expenses are normally charged to the unit contracting the expense, since it is presumed that they will receive the benefit. Where the cost of the expense benefits several cost objectives, it customarily is charged as general and administrative expense and the cost is recognized during the accounting period in which it is incurred.

Professional & Outside Services	*O/H*	*Selling*	*G&A*
Professional services — legal			X
Professional services — accounting and auditing			X
Outside services —			
Repair & maintenance building	X		
Moving & rearranging	X		
Computer	X	X	X
Consultant services			X
Cleaning			X
Clerical	X	X	X

Most of the expenses for utilities and transportation are recorded as overhead, but a portion of them may be reallocated to general and administrative and selling expenses. In the cases of automobile and telephone costs (shown in the following listing), the actual expenses are generally recorded directly to the expense pool that benefits from the expense and no reallocation is necessary.

Utilities & Transportation	O/H	Selling	G&A
Power, heat, fuel, & water	X		
Telephone, telegraph, & teletype	X	X	X
Postage	X		
Freight & cartage	X		
Truck & automobile	X	X	X

The advertising, publicity, and promotion breakdown shown is representative, but the actual breakdown is determined by management according to its need for decision-making information. In many instances this is directly related to particular industries.

Advertising, Publicity, & Promotion	O/H	Selling	G&A
Advertising		X	
Promotional material		X	
Conventions & exhibits		X	
General sales expenses		X	

The cost of travel and business needs and entertainment are recorded and charged to the overhead classifications that generated the expenses. Conferences, dues, and subscriptions are corporate expenses and are therefore included in general and administrative expenses. However, if the operating units have decision-making control over the budgets for these items, then they usually are considered an expense of that overhead classification.

Travel, Conferences, & Memberships	O/H	Selling	G&A
Travel	X	X	X
Business needs	X	X	X
Entertainment			X
Conferences			X
Membership dues & fees			X
Subscription			X

Both employee recruitment and employee welfare expenses are considered costs of the general business operations and are therefore considered to be general and administrative costs. This is generally true if the personnel department has the responsibility for identifying and recruiting staff for the operating units. However, there is some management discretion; if the responsibility for the cost and the control of the budget is assigned to the operating unit, then the expenses can be considered a cost of the operating unit. This is true in many professional service firms where the responsibility for hiring staff is assumed at the operating level. In this instance, when the actual cost of hiring is included in the operating unit overhead, the cost of administrating personnel records by the personnel department would still be included in the general and administrative expense.

Employee Recruitment & Employee Welfare	O/H	Selling	G&A
Interviews & employment expenses			X
Help wanted advertising			X
Relocation expenses			X
Employee relations			X

Occupancy expenses are considered general overhead expenses because they benefit all areas of the company. They are reallocated to the other overhead classifications based on a previously agreed-upon allocation basis.

Occupancy Expenses	O/H	Selling	G&A
Taxes – property	X		
Insurance	X		
Rent – building	X		
Depreciation	X		
Amortization	X		

While all firms and managers prefer not to have a sundry classification, invariably costs are incurred that do not seem to fit any other classification. The accounts shown under the sundry classification below are illustrative of those commonly used.

Sundry	*O/H*	*Selling*	*G&A*
Taxes — state			X
Donations			X
Sundry — other			X

INDIRECT EXPENSES BY TYPE AND BY PURPOSES

In the late 1960s, company managements began to realize that the traditional method of expense classification by type of expense required a significant amount of analysis and reclassification in order to determine the total cost of various operating and management functions. For example, if management wanted to know the cost of conferences for a particular work unit, it was necessary to analyze the travel account to determine how much travel was related to conferences, to break down the labor accounts to reveal the cost of time spent at conferences, and to analyze every account that could possibly have charges related to conferences. In order to arrive at a high degree of confidence in the cost accumulated in this way, it was necessary to completely analyze many accounts.

Management recognized that it wasn't always as important to know the amount of travel costs incurred as it was to know why these costs were incurred and for what purposes. Therefore, the practice of recording expenses by purpose of expense rather than by type of expense was started. Exhibit 3 illustrates how recording expenses by the purpose of the expense interrelates with recording expenses by the type of expense. In order to enable management to know what the costs were through conventional methods of expense accumulation that allow year-to-year cost comparisons to be made, expenses were usually maintained by both methods. To eliminate the need to keep two sets of records, the expenses *by type* were assigned as line items to the expenses *by purpose* (see Exhibit 3).

The following example illustrates the method of recording expenses by both type of expense and purpose of expense. Assume for simplicity that only three accounts by purpose are established and charged during the year — bid and proposal, conference, and office management.

Exhibit 3

Accumulation of Expense by Purpose vs. Type

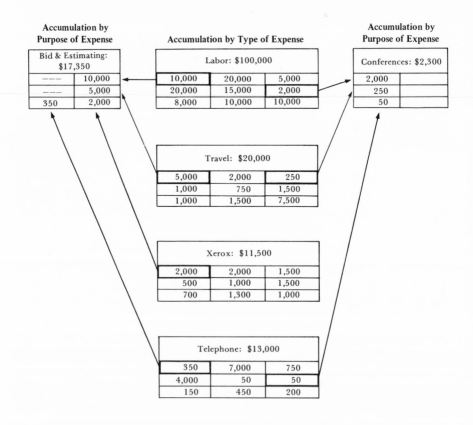

Accumulation by Purpose of Expense

Bid & Estimating: $17,350	
---	10,000
---	5,000
350	2,000

Accumulation by Type of Expense

Labor: $100,000		
10,000	20,000	5,000
20,000	15,000	2,000
8,000	10,000	10,000

Accumulation by Purpose of Expense

Conferences: $2,300	
2,000	
250	
50	

Travel: $20,000		
5,000	2,000	250
1,000	750	1,500
1,000	1,500	7,500

Xerox: $11,500		
2,000	2,000	1,500
500	1,000	1,500
700	1,300	1,000

Telephone: $13,000		
350	7,000	750
4,000	50	50
150	450	200

Office Management Expenses
(by purpose of charge)

Line Item
Number

10	Labor	$10,000	by type of expense
12	Travel	2,000	by type of expense
16	Xerox	1,500	by type of expense
18	Graphics	1,000	by type of expense
20	Telephone	3,000	by type of expense
22	Consultant	500	by type of expense
26	Heat, light, & power	7,000	by type of expense
28	Rent	20,000	by type of expense
30	Outside repairs & maintenance	1,500	by type of expense
	Total	$46,500	by purpose of expense

Bid and Proposal Costs Expense
(by purpose of charge)

Line Item
Number

10	Labor	$10,000	by type of expense
12	Travel (lodging & transportation)	5,000	by type of expense
14	Business needs	500	by type of expense
16	Xerox	500	by type of expense
18	Graphics	1,000	by type of expense
20	Telephone	200	by type of expense
22	Consultants	1,000	by type of expense
	Total bid & proposal costs	$18,200	by purpose of expense

Conference Expenses
(by purpose of charge)

Line Item
Number

10	Labor	$1,000	by type of expense
12	Travel	500	by type of expense
14	Business needs	200	by type of expense
20	Telephone	50	by type of expense
24	Conference (fee for conference)	500	by type of expense
	Total conference cost	$2,250	by purpose of expense

In this type of system, the line items are always the same for a particular type of expense regardless of the account to which they are charged (i.e., labor is always line item 10, telephone is always line item 12, etc.). In order to convert from an accumulation of expense by purpose to an accumulation of expense by type, all like-numbered line items are summarized. Therefore, a time-consuming and costly analysis is not necessary at year end. This is particularly true when data processing equipment is used. The data processing section sorts the costs by line item and prints a summary by types of expense. In practice, the data processing section usually sorts and accumulates the costs by type each month at the same time that costs by purpose of expense are accumulated.

Expense by Purpose

Office management	$46,500
Bid & proposal	18,200
Conference	2,250
Total — All expenses by purpose	$66,950

These same costs accumulated by purpose of expense, when sorted by type of expense, result in the following costs by type of expense:

Expense by Type

Labor	$21,000
Travel	7,500
Business meals	700
Xerox	2,000
Graphics	2,000
Telephone	3,250
Consultants	1,500
Conference	500
Heat, light, & power	7,000
Rent	20,000
Repair & maintenance	1,500
Total — All expenses by type	$66,950

Quite obviously, the total of expenses by purpose and by type must be equal to each other. The segregation of costs by type and by purpose affords management the opportunity to evaluate expenses from two perspectives.

4

Overhead Application

When should overhead be applied? Should it be applied each month with the expense incurred in that month applied specifically to the cost objectives processed through the system during that month? Very few firms do this.

It is recognized that in the overhead expenses recorded within a particular month there are expenses that do not originate in that month. For example, repairs to a machine are charged the month it is fixed; but common sense indicates that the wear and tear that caused the breakdown occurred over a much longer period of time. If the rate were calculated (on a monthly basis) in the month that the expense occurs, then a large expense in that month would have an abnormal effect on the rate and would distort the cost of the project or service in that month.

One possible alternative to monthly rates is to not charge any overhead to the product or service until the financial year is completed and all of the expenses are known. However, this would greatly reduce control over the overhead cost and would hamper management's decision-making ability.

Absorption costing, sometimes called full costing, is a term that is used to describe the extent to which overhead costs are assigned to either a product, a service, or some other cost objective. Absorption costing requires the allocation of these indirect costs to cost objectives, and therefore all expenses are allocated to some cost objective, either directly or indirectly. Most cost accounting systems use absorption costing. Therefore, burden absorption is on an annual basis; all rates are computed on a cumulative basis throughout the fiscal year and are applied retroactively to all products or cost objectives to the beginning of the year. Traditional absorption cost accounting practices do not require assignment of selling or general and administrative expenses to products.

It is normally not practical to use monthly rates, and it is unwieldy to wait until the end of the year, but the use of absorption costs requires that the rate be applied retroactively to all cost objectives to the beginning of the year. Therefore, a method of estimating the year's end rate becomes necessary in order to provide stabilization to cost and to provide management with decision-making information. To overcome this problem, management develops a predetermined overhead rate for the fiscal year. The fiscal year is usually chosen because this period is long enough to average out month-to-month fluctuations and provides a natural cutoff for expenses because the books are closed at this point anyway.

The management of the firm, with the help of the accounting department, projects the rate for the year. During the year, the estimated rate is applied to the actual cost base of each cost objective processed through the firm. Theoretically, at the end of the year, the amount added to the individual cost objectives as overhead should equal the actual expenses accumulated in the overhead account. This never happens. Because the rate used is based on estimated expenses and an estimated base, the actual expense and the actual base will differ. Therefore, the amount that was originally applied to the cost objectives will differ somewhat from the total of the actual expenses.

The sum of the individual charges applied to the cost objectives represents an entry on the debit (left) side of the work-in-process control account or cost-of-goods-sold control account (depending upon the nature of your accounting system). The balancing entry is on the credit (right) side of the account and is called overhead expense applied. The applied expense account is subsequently closed to the actual overhead control account by debiting manufacturing expenses applied and crediting the actual overhead control account. The debit in the actual overhead control account represents the actual expenses incurred during the period.

It should be apparent that the overhead control account collects the actual expenses on the debit side and the applied expenses on the credit side. As mentioned earlier, it is seldom that these two are equal; there is usually a debit or credit balance. If the balance in the overhead control account is a debit the expenses were underapplied and the cost objectives were not allocated enough overhead expense. If the balance in the overhead control account is a credit, the expenses were overapplied and the cost objectives were allocated too much overhead expense. This balance should be analyzed carefully because it is a source of information on the past year's operating efficiency and the reasons why the operational goals of management were missed.

At the end of the year, if the balance (the amount by which the actual expenses are either higher or lower than the applied expenses) in the overhead control account is significant, the accounting department will allocate the balance to all of the cost objectives in the base so that the actual expenses are applied. If the balance is insignificant and there is a debit balance in the account (i.e., the applied amount of expenses is less than the actual expenses), the balance will be added to the cost of goods sold. Or, if there is a credit balance in the account (i.e., the applied amount of expenses was more than the actual expenses), the balance will be subtracted from the cost of goods sold.

The use of T accounts (simply named because of their shape) can best illustrate, step-by-step, how applied overhead works.

A. Each month the projected overhead is applied to individual cost objectives and the summary entry is charged to the cost of goods sold.

Costs of Goods Sold		Applied Overhead Control	
A) 250,000			A) 250,000

B. Each month the actual overhead expenses are summarized in the actual overhead account.

Actual Overhead Control Account		Cash	
B) 270,000			B) 270,000

C. At the end of the year, the applied overhead account is closed to the actual overhead control account.

Actual Overhead Control Account		Applied Overhead Control Account	
B) 270,000	C) 250,000	C) 250,000	A) 250,000

D. The balance in the actual overhead control account is distributed equitably among the individual cost objectives and written off to cost of goods sold.

Cost of Goods Sold		Actual Overhead Control Account	
A) 250,000		B) 270,000	C) 250,000
D) 20,000			D) 20,000
270,000		270,000	270,000

The variance illustrated would be reallocated to individual cost objectives. However, as indicated earlier, if the variance between applied and actual overhead is small, the write-off is made directly to the cost of goods sold without distribution among the individual cost objectives. The determination as to what is small will vary, but, as a general rule, if the allocation of the over- or underapplied cost will have a signficant effect on the cost of any cost objective, then the variance should be allocated.

5

Projecting Predetermined Overhead Rates

The method of projecting the predetermined overhead rate varies from company to company and ranges from a very simple approach in very small firms to larger, sophisticated projection systems in very large firms. The methods and degrees of difficulty are also affected by the general economic outlook of the company, the industry, and the nation; by the competitive nature of the industry; and according to whether the firm is planning large growth in that year or approximately the same level of operations as the year before. Regardless of the method or the detail involved, there are five steps common to all projection systems:

1. determination of the year/period involved
2. estimation of the indirect expenses for the year/period
3. projection of the estimated volume for the year/period
4. determination of the expected base that will result from the expected volume of business for the year/period
5. calculation of the predictive rate by dividing the projected indirect expense by the expected base

PROJECTION PERIOD

The period generally accepted is the fiscal year because it provides a natural cutoff for expenses and because it is long enough to ensure that seasonal variations or other short-term effects do not overly distort the rate calculations. The period does not have to coincide with contract performance, but the projection period must exactly coincide with the expenses that are being accumulated in the overhead accounts.

ESTIMATION OF OVERHEAD EXPENSES

The first step in estimating the overhead expenses is to evaluate the pattern of behavior of the expenses. This is done by reviewing past cost performance to gain knowledge of the size and the patterns of the individual expenses. It is generally found that certain expenses remain about the same from period to period. Other expenses will change as production or volume of work performed changes. The expenses can easily be divided into two major classifications — fixed expenses and variable expenses.

A fixed expense is one whose amount remains constant in the short-term regardless of the volume of work performed. Examples of fixed expenses are rent, depreciation of real estate, taxes, and insurance. These expenses remain the same whether no work or a full capacity of work is performed. If we assume that the business will continue, the rent and the depreciation allowance for the equipment will continue, even at zero production or zero volume of work. However, this definition holds true only if the normal capacity of the operation is not changed. Expansion of the firm, which will result in increased rent, or purchase of new equipment will cause an increase in these expenses.

The balance of the expenses is classified as variable expenses. A variable expense is one whose amount changes directly in proportion to changes in production or work level. Increases in work cause corresponding increases in variable expenses. Without production or work there would theoretically be no variable expenses and therefore no cost. Examples of variable expenses are supplies, power, and electricity.

A close inspection of the patterns and behavior of the overhead expenses quickly leads to the conclusion that all expenses do not stay fixed as production increases, nor do they vary directly with the amount of work performed. In other words, a portion of the expenses acts like a fixed expense and a portion of the expenses acts like a variable expense. These expenses vary with production but do not do so directly. They are known as semivariable expenses and the majority of expenses fall into this classification. Examples of this expense type include the salary of the quality control supervisor, office supplies, and telephone costs.

After reviewing the patterns and behavior of expenses, management must assign them to the three classes — fixed, variable, or semivariable. The above discussion oversimplifies a difficult process. The splitting of the expenses into fixed and variable may not be difficult. However, it should be pointed out that the categorization of cost is not always cut-and-dry. For example, expenses that would be variable in one industry can be fixed in another.

A chemical plant produces its output by processing raw material through its system. All of the staff, including the inspectors and supervisors, is necessary for the plant to operate at all. In preparing its budget, this company treats the normally variable expenses of the inspector and supervisor as a fixed cost.

Within a particular firm it is not normally difficult to divide costs into the fixed and variable categories. However, many costs have both fixed and variable components, and to segregate them into their elements is very difficult.

Although budgeting is beyond the scope or intent of this book, a couple of methods are reviewed so that they will be familiar. One of the simplest approaches used in manufacturing is the high-low method, in which the past cost data is reviewed and the units produced are listed in order from the lowest units produced to the highest. (See Exhibit 4.) On the basis of this information, the cost of inspection can vary as much as $ .02 per production unit. From this information, the fixed portion of the expense can be determined. The bottom portion of Exhibit 4 shows that the cost of inspection was established as a constant increase. In most cases this will not be a uniform increase, but the procedure used will be the same. The total increase in the expenses is divided by the total increase in production to obtain an average variable cost per unit. The average variable unit cost is then multiplied by the units of production each month to get the total variable portion of the expense. This is then subtracted from the total cost to obtain the fixed portion. This

Exhibit 4

High-Low Method

	Units of Production	Cost of Inspection
January	200,000	$14,000
February	210,000	14,200
March	230,000	14,650
April	240,000	14,800
May	180,000	13,600
June	170,000	13,400
July	150,000	13,000
August	140,000	12,800
September	225,000	14,500
October	250,000	15,000
November	245,000	14,900
December	220,000	14,400
Total	2,460,000	$169,250

	Units of Production	Cost of Inspection	Units of Production	Increase in Cost of Inspection
August	140,000	$12,800	$ —	$ —
July	150,000	13,000	10,000	200
June	170,000	13,400	20,000	400
May	180,000	13,600	10,000	200
January	200,000	14,000	20,000	400
February	210,000	14,200	10,000	200
December	220,000	14,400	10,000	200
September	225,000	14,500	5,000	100
March	230,000	14,600	5,000	100
April	240,000	14,800	10,000	200
November	245,000	14,900	5,000	100
October	250,000	15,000	5,000	100
			$110,000	$ 2,200

$$\frac{\$2,200}{110,000 \text{ units}} = \$.02 \text{ per unit}$$

Units of Production	2% of Variable Cost per Unit	Total Cost	Fixed Amount
140,000	$2,800	$12,800	$10,000 ($12,800 − $2,800)
150,000	3,000	13,000	10,000 (13,000 − 3,000)
170,000	3,400	13,400	10,000 (13,400 − 3,400)
180,000	3,600	13,600	10,000 (13,600 − 3,600)
200,000	4,000	14,000	10,000 (14,000 − 4,000)
210,000	4,200	14,200	10,000 (14,200 − 4,200)
220,000	4,400	14,400	10,000 (14,400 − 4,400)

ETC.

illustration provides a clear picture of the effect that an increase in production has on increasing the variable portion of a semivariable expense.

The difficulties with the high-low method are that:

it is particularly valuable only to manufacturing firms,

it is time-consuming to develop for all costs, and

a clear relationship between the costs is not always evident.

It is clear that the high-low method would not work in a service industry where there are no measurable production units. The typical service organization uses other methods. One such method used by service firms is to estimate the fixed portion of the expense both at zero level of operation and at the expected level of operation. By drawing a graph and connecting these two points, a sloping line is developed, which represents the variable portion of the expense.

For example, if the cost of supervising an engineering office is $300,000 a year for $1,200,000 of engineering direct labor and management believes that $100,000 of supervision is fixed or would be necessary even if operations neared zero level, then the variable costs would be calculated as follows:

$$\frac{\$\ 200,000}{\$1,200,000} = 16.67\%$$

This means that the supervisory cost at any volume (X) will be $100,000 + .1667 of direct labor at volume X. Exhibit 5 presents a graph that demonstrates this method.

An advantage of this system is its simplicity. Its main disadvantage is that the range of direct labor could be very wide (i.e., $0 − 1,200,000 in the example). Most overhead costs are not linear from zero volume to actual operating costs.

A third method expands upon the simplicity of the second method. In this approach, the total cost of the projected expense is estimated at two levels of effort. In such a graph, a line is drawn between the two points and extended to zero. The slope of the line between the two points represents the variable cost of the expense at different production or operational levels.

Exhibit 5

Variable Portion of Expense Derived by Use of a 2-Plot Graph

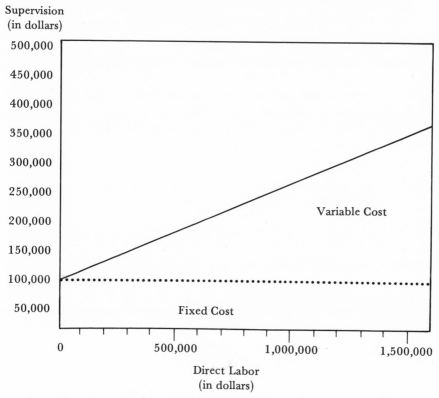

Supervision
(in dollars)

Direct Labor
(in dollars)

For example, assume that management can estimate that direct labor will be between $1,000,000 and $1,500,000 but anticipates that it will be close to $1,200,000. The supervision costs are estimated to be $325,000 at the $1,000,000 direct labor level and $400,000 when direct labor is at the $1,500,000 level. The variable cost rate would be calculated as follows:

	Supervision	*Direct Labor*
$1,500,000 level	$400,000	$1,500,000
$1,000,000 level	−325,000	−1,000,000
	$ 75,000	$ 500,000

$$\text{Variable cost rate} \quad \frac{\$\ 75,000}{\$500,000} = .15 = 15\%$$

Fixed costs = Total supervision costs @ $1,000,000 minus variable cost @ $1,000,000 level or $325,000 − ($1,000,000 x .15) = $175,000

The advantage of this method is that the variable rate is calculated over the range that is most likely to occur. The graph in Exhibit 6 illustrates this method.

Both of these methods use two points to calculate the variable rate on a graph. Another method (which will not be illustrated)

Exhibit 6

Fixed Portion of Expense Derived From 3-Plot Graph

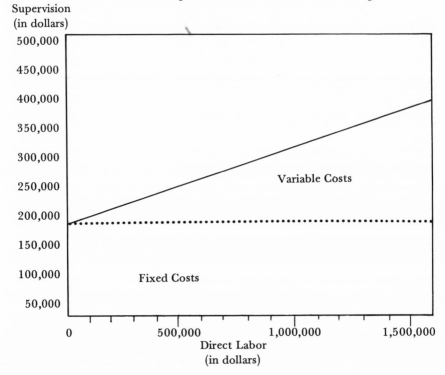

Supervision (in dollars) vs. Direct Labor (in dollars)

uses actual historical data. The data is plotted on a graph as a straight line, either by inspection or by statistical calculations. This method has the advantage of having many points plotted. (The greater the number of points plotted, the less the effect of distortion in the variable rate.) The greater disadvantage of this method is that it may build into the variable rate inefficiencies from prior operation.

It should be evident that, unless a good linear relationship exists between the base and the expense reviewed, distortion results. These methods use linear relationships to plot items that are never a linear function. Almost all costs are curvilinear, that is, the rate of change is different at different volume levels.

It should also be pointed out that many firms do not go to the detail of splitting the semivariable expenses into the fixed and variable portions. In cases where this is done, it is usually accomplished by using a superficial method because of the cost and time involved. Imagine a large firm with 15 operating departments, each having 50 semivariable expense classifications. Such a firm would require the analysis of 750 accounts (50 x 15). Where it is decided to split these semivariables into their fixed and variable portions, it would most likely be done empirically using a graphic method with only two points plotted. In a very large operation, even this amount of analysis could be costly and would take a large amount of time. There are four important items to remember, namely: (1) there is no right or wrong way to calculate rates — the method that best enables management to estimate its overhead expenses for the next year is correct; (2) all methods provide only approximations; (3) a constant relationship must exist among the components of the cost being reviewed in order to lessen the problem of distortion; and (4) the method chosen should be as simple as possible, should give reasonable results, and should be easily understood by line management.

DETERMINATION OF BASE

The great number of methods available to forecast volume levels are beyond the scope of this work and will not be considered. Each firm chooses the method that best fits its needs. However, the importance that the volume chosen has on the estimated expense and projected base should be stressed. It is important to select a volume level that reflects the reasonable capacity of the firm, that considers the economic outlook of the economy and the industry, and that can be obtained with available resources.

Once the period has been chosen and the overhead expenses have been forecasted, then the base on which the expenses are going to be allocated is chosen and forecasted. Good accounting and management practices dictate that the base must be consistent from year to year. For purposes of demonstration, several bases will be reviewed. While several bases are available, probably the most accurate and the one predominantly used is direct labor dollars. However, also considered here are: the unit of production basis, the material cost basis, the machine hour basis, the total direct cost basis, the direct labor hour basis, and the direct labor cost basis.

Unit of Production Basis

The unit of production basis is probably the simplest and the most direct method of applying overhead expenses. The estimated overhead expenses are divided by the estimated unit of production to calculate an expense per unit. As shown below, the estimated expenses of $300,000 are divided by 250,000, the number of units planned for production during the next year.

$$\frac{\text{estimated overhead expenses}}{\text{estimated units of production}} = \frac{\text{amount of expense}}{\text{per unit}}$$

$$\frac{\$300,000}{250,000} = \$1.20$$

As each unit is completed, it will be charged overhead of $1.20 as its share of the overhead expenses. Therefore, a cost objective with 100,000 units completed would receive an allocation of $120,000 overhead expense (100,000 x $1.20 = $120,000). This is a satisfactory procedure when the company only produces one product. But if the company produces more than one product, this cost allocation is incorrect. In addition, if the products vary in size or require different amounts of material or time to produce, this method results in incorrect costing.

Materials Cost Basis

The material cost basis is used where a company has found that there is a direct correlation between the materials used in the product and the overhead expenses. The study might show that the overhead expenses remain about the same percentage of direct material all the time. Therefore, the estimated manufacturing expenses are divided by the estimated material costs and are then multiplied by 100 to get a rate. This would be expressed as a percentage of overhead expense per direct material dollar. If the material were estimated to be $400,000 and the estimated overhead expense were $500,000, a rate of 126 percent would be calculated for the next accounting period.

$$\frac{\text{estimated overhead expenses}}{\text{estimated material costs}} \times 100 = \begin{array}{l}\text{percentage of}\\\text{expense per direct}\\\text{material dollar}\end{array}$$

$$\frac{\$500,000}{\$400,000} \times 100 = 125\% \text{ or } \$1.25 \text{ per direct material dollar}$$

This means that, for every dollar of material charged to the cost objective, there would be $1.25 worth of overhead. Or, if the materials in a cost objective cost $5,000, then the overhead would cost $6,250. This approach is only logical if the relationship remains constant. If there were two or three products, and one was fabricated with very expensive material and the others composed of something less expensive, the product with the high material costs would absorb a disproportionate share of the overhead expense. This would be particularly true if the products all shared the same fabrication process and required approximately the same amount of processing. They should share equally in the overhead allocation.

Machine Hour Basis

The machine hour method is based on the time required to operate each machine or group of machines in performing identical operations. The number of machine hours employed is estimated and the hourly rate is determined by the following formula:

$$\frac{\text{estimated overhead expenses}}{\text{estimated machine hours}} = \text{rate per machine hour}$$

If it is assumed that 300,000 machine hours will be employed, and the estimated expenses are $300,000, then the rate is $1.00, and is calculated as follows:

$$\frac{\$300,000}{300,000} = \$1.00$$

Therefore, if a cost objective required 350 machine hours, it would be charged $350 for overhead expenses. This method requires additional clerical work because someone like a shop foreman has to collect the machine information that will permit the charging of the cost objective by the hours expended on the machine.

Total Direct Cost Basis

The total direct cost method is used by consulting firms rather than manufacturing firms. The Commonwealth of Pennsylvania used only this method for reimbursing consultants until 1970. This method summarizes all of the direct prime costs, labor, and material and divides the total into the estimated overhead expenses.

$$\frac{\text{estimated overhead expenses}}{\text{total direct costs}} = \text{rate per dollar of direct costs}$$

For example, if the overhead expenses were projected at $300,000 and the total direct costs were $600,000, composed of $250,000 direct labor and $350,000 materials, then the rate would be $.50 per direct cost dollar, calculated as follows:

$$\frac{\$300,000}{\$600,000} = \$ \ .50$$

Direct Labor Hour Basis

The computation of this rate is based on the following formula:

$$\frac{\text{estimated overhead expense}}{\text{estimate direct labor hours}} = \text{rate per direct labor hour}$$

For illustrative purposes, assume that the direct labor hours are estimated at 200,000 for the coming period and the cost of overhead expenses are estimated at $300,000. For every hour charged direct, $1.50 of overhead would be applied, computed as follows:

$$\frac{\$300,000}{200,000} = \$1.50$$

A cost objective having 400 hours of direct labor would be charged with $600 of overhead. This method, although one of the most accurate and fair, requires extra work because direct labor hours must be summarized. However, in a manufacturing firm, where there is heavy machine usage that contributes more to the production of the final product than the labor hours do, this method may not yield the most equitable basis. This disadvantage is overcome by using the machine hour method.

Direct Labor Dollars Basis

Probably the earliest, oldest, and most predominant method of applying overhead to cost objective is the direct labor cost basis, formulated in the following way:

$$\frac{\text{estimated overhead expenses}}{\text{estimated direct labor}} \times 100 = \text{percentage of direct labor}$$

If we assume that the amount of overhead expense is $300,000 and the estimated direct labor is $300,000, a rate of 100 percent is developed. This is an easy-to-use system, both because most of the information is available from the general accounting records and because it is information that already has to be collected to satisfy government statutes.

Most overhead expenses are consumed on a time basis. Power, light, rent, etc., are used on a time basis. Therefore, the method used should take this time factor into consideration. The direct labor dollar method fulfills the time requirements because the time labor cost of the cost objective is computed by multiplying the number of hours spent times the wage of the person. The more hours spent on the job, the higher the labor cost and the greater the overhead cost.

The great disadvantage of this base is that the total labor hour cost represents the sum of the high- and the low-wage worker. By applying overhead on the basis of direct labor cost, a cost objective is charged with more overhead when a high-rate person works on it than when a low-rate person does. Such a method could lead to incorrect distribution of overhead if numerous operators with different hourly rates perform on a contract. However, it is universally agreed that direct labor is the easiest and overall the most equitable basis to use.

PREDETERMINED RATE CALCULATION

Once the expenses have been estimated and the base has been projected, by taking the anticipated operating level into consideration, a predetermined rate can be calculated. The projected rate is calculated by dividing the projected overhead by the projected base. This rate is applied to the incurred cost on a cumulative basis each month or accounting period. For each operating period, there will be a difference between the overhead costs generated by applying the predetermined rate and the actual overhead costs. In some firms, the difference is "written off" or recorded on an account called over- or underapplied overhead. The cumulative balance in this account is transferred to the profit and loss summary. This method is particularly useful when the difference between applied and actual overhead is a fairly stable or constant amount throughout a year.

If the amount applied as overhead is greater than the actual overhead, then the balance in the over- or underapplied overhead account is a credit (right side) balance and results in a positive effect on profit. If the applied overhead is less than the actual overhead cost, the balance in the over- or underapplied overhead account is a debit (left side) balance and has a negative effect on profit. Review the cost information for the Arco manufacturing firm:

Through Month	Applied Cumulative Overhead	Actual Cumulative Overhead	Cumulative Over- or Underapplied
1	$100,000	$ 90,000	$ (10,000)
2	150,000	160,000	10,000
3	220,000	215,000	(5,000)
4	270,000	282,000	12,000

At the end of the 4th accounting period, the Arco manufacturing had underapplied its overhead expenses. When the balance is closed out to profit and loss, it will have a negative effect on profit.

The following entries would be made each accounting period to the over- or underapplied overhead account in order to reflect the proper balance in the account.

Month	Debit	Credit
1		$10,000
2	$20,000	
3		$15,000
4	$17,000	

Remember the cost presented was cumulative cost; therefore, the entries have to reflect the difference between successive balances. In other words, to go from a cumulative balance of $15,000 credit to a debit balance of $10,000 requires that the account be debited with $25,000. Based on the above entries, the over- and underapplied account would look like the following:

Month	Debit	Credit	Balance Over/ Under Account Debit (Credit)
1		$10,000	$(10,000)
2	$20,000		10,000
3		$15,000	(5,000)
4	$17,000		12,000

It was stated that, as long as the difference between applied over-head and actual overhead was not significant, the above approach was used. However, if there is a great variation in the cost charged monthly to overhead during the account year, the difference between applied and actual could be significant. In a seasonal busi-ness the actual overhead costs may be high in relation to the base in the slack period, whereas the actual overhead costs may be low relative to the base during the peak business cycle. These wide fluctuations may net out so that the predetermined rate would be correct at year-end but would cause wide distortion to the profit picture if the difference between actual and applied overhead was considered within the accounting period.

It would be incorrect to reflect heavy losses during one part of the year (because the actual rate is higher than the anticipated year-end rate) and inflated profit during the balance of the year (when the rate is low relative to the projected year-end rate). In order to compensate for seasonal variations or widely fluctuating rates, man-agement will apply predetermined (forecasted) rates and reclassify the variance between applied overhead and actual overhead as long as it is confident that the predetermined rate will be met at year-end. During the period when the actual overhead costs are greater than the applied overhead costs (but the year-end rate is still antici-pated), the difference between the applied and actual overhead is classified on the balance sheet as a debit to deferred costs. This recognizes that those costs will offset the cost in the period when the costs will be low relative to the base. Alternatively, during the periods when the actual overhead cost is less than the applied overhead costs (but the predetermined year-end rate is still anticipated), the variance is classified on the balance sheet as a deferred credit. When the seasonal swing takes place and the overhead costs are high relative to the base, this account will be reduced to zero. The important fact to recognize is that this transfer should only be made when management is sure that the year-end predetermined rates will be realized. In many practical instances, rather than being shown as a deferred cost or deferred credit, the variance is reflected through the inventory account. If the predetermined (forecasted) rates are not expected to be realized, the adjustment should definitely be through the inventory account. Any significant variance from the planned rates should be reflected in the cost as soon as they are anticipated.

6

Departmental or Cost Center Overhead

Thus far, the projection of a predetermined rate, the application of that rate to actual cost, and the write-off of the variance between the actual and the applied overhead costs to cost of goods sold have been considered. This type of predetermined rate is known as a blanket rate because it is a single rate that is used for all cost objectives.

In actual practice, large firms use departmental or cost center rates rather than blanket rates. These multiple rates are predetermined by the cost center, and a separate burden rate is created for each cost center. Dividing the operation into separate departments or cost centers ensures better control over the overhead costs and provides more accurate costing of contracts, products, or services.

One aim of management is always to obtain better control of expenditures in order to reduce cost. It is difficult, however, to reduce the costs of direct labor and material. But by exercising stricter control over expenses, it is possible to reduce overhead.

Breaking the overhead rate into cost centers provides for better control because it places specific responsibility on each cost center manager for a limited range of expenses. Also, more accurate costing of contracts, products, and services is possible because departmentalization leads to the use of different burden rates for applying overhead expense. A contract, product, or service processed through a department or cost center is charged with that department's rate. Thus, if all contracts, products, or services are not processed through every department in the firm, they absorb only the rates of the departments they are processed through and management receives better costing data. The use of one rate would be inaccurate if a product only went through certain departments but was charged with the manufacturing expenses of the overall firm.

The process of departmentalizing the overhead expense into separate overhead rates is an extension of the previous overhead rate discussion. The overall steps are the same, but are more detailed. It is necessary to estimate the expense (by cost centers instead of the entire firm), to determine the proper base (the same base should be chosen for all cost centers within the operation), to maintain general ledger control over the cost centers' expenses (there is a general ledger control account for each cost center as there was for the firm when using only one rate), and to compute the variance between the applied and the actual expenses. (The over- and under-applied overhead accounts are maintained by cost center instead of being one figure for the entire firm.) By breaking the rates into cost centers, the variance between applied and actual expenses provides an even better understanding of the cause for the variance and simplifies cost analysis because management has more refined or detailed data at its disposal.

The organization of overhead rates by cost center is a very important but somewhat arbitrary procedure that varies from firm to firm. The cost centers are determined by management after consideration of the following questions:

1. What cost centers will provide the best overhead control?
2. What cost centers will provide the most accurate cost allocation to the final cost objectives?
3. What cost centers most logically fit the organization?

4. What form of cost center organization is the easiest to accomplish?

5. What approach provides the best cost/benefit relationship?

6. What other alternatives are there?

There are no hard and fast rules. The following are some of the methods used to group activities into cost centers:

the grouping of the product/client services, such as grouping the cost centers according to final product or client service performed (the product/service approach);

the grouping together of like disciplinary functions, such as design engineers, component engineers, product engineers, or field service engineers — all engineers (a function performed approach);

the grouping of the cost center according to formal organization, such as grouping all of the functions reporting to one supervisor into a cost center (the organizational approach).

Management makes its decision on which approach to use so that the most logical and cost-effective system is available to provide the best expense control and the most accurate allocation of cost. The more varied or complicated the product or service, the more detailed the overhead structure must be in order to provide accurate costing. But the overhead structure should not be made more complicated or detailed than necessary if a more precise but simpler method would provide the same basic results.

In order to use multiple rates, the firm must divide the operation into production and service departments. The production department in a manufacturing firm is involved in the actual fabrication of the product; in a service organization work performed for the client or customer is involved. The service department within any organization renders a service to both the production and other service departments. Examples of production departments in a manufacturing firm are the cutting department, the machining department, or the assembly department. A store's inventory, production control, and maintenance departments are examples of service departments.

All overhead expenses are either direct or indirect expenses of the cost centers. Those expenses that are under the control of the supervisor of the cost center immediately upon occurrence are charged immediately to the cost center. This applies to production departments as well as to service departments. The types of expenses that are generally closely related to the operation of a cost center are supervision, indirect supplies, and indirect materials.

There are also expenses that do not originate in the individual cost center but that apply to the firm as a unit and must be prorated to the production and service departments on some equitable basis. Classified as general expenses, these include real estate taxes and depreciation on the building and are shared by all cost centers. Determining a fair method for allocating these general expenses requires a great deal of careful study and planning to be sure that the distribution is equitable. While the selection of the basis for prorating is difficult in many cases, it is a management decision that is negotiated among cost centers.

For example, management could allocate the total economic rental cost, which could include the cost of rent, depreciation on the building, utilities, insurance, etc., on a square footage basis. However, certain departments, such as production control or stores with rooms that have ten-foot ceilings may argue that the operating plant area which has very high ceilings should be allocated a greater share of the economic rent. A discussion would then be held among the managers of the departments as well as the accounting or budgeting departments and a possible alternative might be worked out that would use cubic footage in order to provide a more equitable basis.

It is a matter of equity. Determining the base and selling it to the line managers generally leads to a great deal of discussion and review before finalization. All possible methods of prorations are not discussed here, but Exhibit 7 reflects some of the expenses that are commonly prorated and the bases that are usually used. Before attempting to prorate expenses, some very accurate allocation information must be gathered; it should never be estimated. A survey should be made to collect the necessary data.

The general steps in rate calculation outlined previously for the blanket rate can now be clearly defined in 8 steps for cost center rate calculations.

1. Define the cost centers.
2. Define the overhead base for rate calculation.
3. Collect the direct costs by cost center and the indirect costs in a general overhead account.
4. Collect data to support the prorations.
5. Prorate the general expenses to the various cost centers on the basis determined in Step 4.
6. Prorate the service departments to the production departments.
7. Add the reallocations to the direct cost center expenses to arrive at an adjusted overhead expense.
8. Calculate cost center rates by dividing the adjusted cost center overhead by the base in Step 2.

To assist in clarifying the above steps, an overhead rate calculation schedule is provided for review in Exhibit 8. Each step in the allocation and rate calculation process has been followed.

Define the Cost Centers

The EZ Manufacturing Company uses seven production departments — fabrication, cutting, plotting, machining, drilling, assembly, and finishing; three service departments — stores, production control, and maintenance; and one account to collect the general overhead expenses.

Define the Overhead Base

A review of Exhibit 8 indicates that direct labor involved in the production is the base used for rate calculation by the EZ Manufacturing Company. In this example, the direct labor summarized from the time sheets of the production workers amounts to $1,062,000.

Collect Direct and Indirect Expenses

Exhibit 8 also reflects the breakdown of the direct overhead expenses charged to the cost centers as taken from the individual

Exhibit 7

Expenses and Their Common Allocation Base

Expense	*Allocation Base*
Telephone & telegraph	Number of employees
Light	Kilowatt hours
Power	Horsepower hours
Rent	Square or cubic footage
Repairs & maintenance	Square footage/number of machines
Supervision	Number of people
Freight in	Direct material
Shop supplies	Direct labor
Small tools	Direct labor
Inspection labor	Direct labor
Depreciation on building	Square footage
Property tax & insurance	Square footage or value of equipment assigned
Taxes	Book value assigned
Industrial relation & personnel	Number of people
Plant supervision	Departmental direct labor
Accounting	Relative value of products

overhead control account. It also reflects the cost by type of expense collected in the general overhead account. The second column of the rate schedule is departmental overhead of both production and service departments as taken from the general ledger control accounts. This amounts to $1,096,000. Included in this amount is the overhead collected in the general overhead account, which reflects the cost by type of expense. The types of expenses included can be seen by reviewing the line called general expense. The overhead in this column is sometimes referred to as controllable overhead because it is under the control of the supervisors of each department.

Exhibit 8

EZ Manufacturing Company Departmental Overhead Rate Schedule

	Direct labor	Departmental overhead	Labor additives/ benefits	Indirect materials & supplies	Light	Power	Occupancy expense	Plant supervision	General expenses (balance)	Maintenance	Production control	Stores	Total allocated overhead	Departmental overhead
Fabrication	$212,000	$ 75,000	$ 71,100	$ 5,990	$ 3,000	$ 4,000	$60,000	$ 7,200	$14,196	$ 2,594	$16,897	$45,158	$305,135	143.93%
Cutting	190,000	70,000	59,400	5,365	2,000	7,500	15,000	6,000	11,860	1,300	14,074	4,516	197,015	103.69%
Plating	80,000	15,000	26,400	2,260	2,000	4,000	30,000	3,000	5,271	18,160	7,037	9,032	122,160	152.70%
Machining	150,000	20,000	48,600	4,235	8,000	12,000	39,000	5,400	9,704	103,764	12,672	4,516	267,891	178.59%
Drilling	70,000	20,000	24,000	1,980	6,000	8,500	15,000	2,700	4,792	38,898	6,337	4,516	132,723	189.60%
Assembly	300,000	90,000	108,000	8,475	2,000	2,000	120,000	13,500	21,564	2,594	31,664	18,064	417,861	139.29%
Finishing	60,000	12,000	20,400	1,695	4,000	2,000	31,500	2,700	4,073	2,594	6,337	4,516	90,315	150.53%
Stores	—	48,000	14,400	—	1,000	500	18,000	1,500	2,876	522	3,520	(90,318)	—	—
Production control	—	48,000	14,400	—	1,000	500	30,000	1,500	2,876	262	(98,538)		—	—
Maintenance	—	120,000	36,000	—	1,000	500	1,500	4,500	7,188	(170,688)			—	—
General expenses	—	578,000	14,400	(30,000)	(30,000)	(40,000)	(360,000)	(48,000)	(84,400)				—	—
Total	$1,062,000	$1,096,000	$437,100	–0–	–0–	–0–	–0–	–0–	–0–	–0–	–0–	–0–	$1,533,100	144.36%
Basis of distribution	—	—	Benefit rate time department labor	Direct labor	Kilowatt hours	Horse-power hours	Square footage	Number of employees	Total department labor	Value of equipment	Number of employees	Direct material	—	—

Many firms include their surcharges, labor additives, or fringe benefits (all are the same thing) in the labor rates. Other firms accumulate the fringe benefits in one pool and allocate them on the rate schedule. The two methods are equally acceptable. In the case of the EZ Manufacturing Company, a 30 percent fringe rate was developed. This rate is multiplied by the direct and indirect production labor of the production departments and the labor in the service departments (including the staff people assigned to the general overhead area), as shown in Exhibit 9.

Collect Data to Support Basis of Proration

Exhibit 10 is the result of a survey of the EZ Manufacturing plant. The information gained from the survey is used to distribute costs in the general overhead account and to reallocate the service departments to the other production cost centers.

Exhibit 9

Calculation of Fringe Based on 30 Percent of Total Labor

	Direct Labor	Indirect Labor	Total Labor	Labor Addition @ 30%
Fabrication	$212,000	$ 25,000	$237,000	$ 71,100
Cutting	190,000	8,000	198,000	59,400
Plating	80,000	8,000	88,000	26,400
Machining	150,000	12,000	162,000	48,600
Drilling	70,000	10,000	80,000	24,000
Assembly	300,000	60,000	360,000	108,000
Finishing	60,000	8,000	68,000	20,400
Stores	—	48,000	48,000	14,400
Production control	—	48,000	48,000	14,400
Maintenance	—	120,000	120,000	36,000
General overhead	—	48,000	48,000	14,400
Total	$1,062,000	$395,000	$1,457,000	$437,100

Exhibit 10

Staff Survey

	Kilowatt Hours Used	Horsepower Used	Square Footage	Number of Employees	Equipment Costs	Direct Material
Fabrication	3,000	8,000	20,000	24	$ 10,000	$ 50,000
Cutting	2,000	15,000	5,000	20	5,000	5,000
Plating	2,000	8,000	10,000	10	70,000	10,000
Machining	8,000	24,000	13,000	18	400,000	5,000
Drilling	6,000	17,000	5,000	9	150,000	5,000
Assembly	2,000	4,000	40,000	45	10,000	20,000
Finishing	4,000	1,000	10,500	9	10,000	5,000
Stores	1,000	1,000	6,000	5	2,000	—
Production control	1,000	1,000	10,000	5	1,000	—
Maintenance	1,000	1,000	500	15	1,000	—
General expense	1,000	1,000	500	5	—	—
Subtotal	31,000	81,000	120,500	165	$659,000	$100,000
Less general expense	−1,000	−1,000	− 500	− 5	—	
Base for distribution	30,000	80,000	120,000	160	$659,000	
Less maintenance				−15	− 1,000	
Base for distribution				145	$658,000	
Less production control				− 5		
Base for distribution				140		

Prorate the General Expenses

The next column is indirect materials and supplies and marks the beginning of the distribution of the general overhead expense. This expense is allocated only to those areas that use it. Stores, production control, maintenance, and general expenses do not share in this expense. It is distributed based on direct labor, on the assumption that the supplies, which are small consumable items, are included in the final product by the people in the production line.

The next distribution of general expense is the expense for lights. The factory survey indicated that 31,000 kilowatt hours were used. The amount used by the general overhead people was eliminated from the total used and the balance was distributed to the production and service areas.

The next column is the expense for power and this was based on horsepower used. Again, it was, just like the expense for light usage, redistributed to all service and production areas after eliminating the horsepower used by the general overhead staff. (See staff survey, Exhibit 10.)

The next column is the expense for occupany, which is the economic rent of these departments. It includes the general rent, general taxes, real estate taxes, and general insurance on the building as well as depreciation on the building. It is distributed based on the square footage of the areas using the space. Although general overhead staff occupies some area, that space has been eliminated for distribution purposes.

The next column is plant supervision. Plant supervision is located in the general overhead account and is distributed based on the number of employees, less those in the general overhead account.

The last distribution of expenses from general overhead expense is the balance of the general overhead expense. It has been distributed based on total cost center labor, on the assumption that most of the balance of the expenses in that account was related to staff functions and, therefore, the total labor costs of both direct and indirect people in all of the production and service areas benefited from the expense. (See Exhibit 10.)

The general overhead account shows the departmental expenses sum of $578,000 plus the $14,400 of labor employee benefits equal to the amount of credits distributed from that department. Thus, there is no more cost retaining in that control account.

Prorate the Service Departments

The service departments should be studied carefully to determine the best method for distributing their expenses to the production departments. The rate for the cost centers is calculated only after this distribution has been made. There are rules that should be applied in making the distribution of the service expenses to the production departments. The first rule is that the service department expenses are transferred to the production departments according to the use made by those production departments of the service departments.

This requires a decision regarding which service department should be closed out first because, while production departments receive service from the service departments, other service departments are serviced by them as well. Thus, instead of closing out the expenses of each service department directly to the production departments, a process of charging out the service departments' costs to both the production and the other service departments is necessary. This difficulty is overcome by distributing the service department that renders the greatest amount of service first and then the other service departments in turn. In some cases, it is not an easy task to determine the exact amount of service rendered by one department to another. When the service rendered cannot be measured accurately, another rule is followed: Prorate the department with the largest total expenses first. This rule assumes that the largest amount of expense provides the greatest amount of service.

For any base used in making a distribution, it is necessary to eliminate from that base the amount that pertains to the department whose expenses are being distributed. In other words, distribution is made on the total amount that pertains to the departments receiving the allocation. For example, in the production control department, expenses of $95,400 are distributed on the basis of 155, which is the total after deducting the five people in the production control department. (Total people — 160 — less 5 assigned to production control department equals 155.)

To summarize the rules for distribution of service department expenses, the largest or most used service department is distributed first, the costs are reallocated to both production and service departments, and the portion of the base of the service department being distributed should be eliminated before distribution.

In this illustration, it is clear that maintenance provides the greatest amount of service because all of the areas, both production and service, receive maintenance services from this department. This cost is distributed based on the equipment costs assigned to each cost center. (See Exhibit 10.) Since the maintenance department does have some equipment, this again is eliminated before making the distribution. All of the cost of maintenance has been redistributed and the balance in the account is zero.

After the maintenance department, the production control department provides the next greatest service. They not only provide service to all the production departments, but they maintain the control accounts for the remaining service department — stores. Production control is distributed based on the number of people, except the employees, in the production control department. Reading across production control, the amount that is redistributed is the sum of departmental expenses, labor additives, and their share of light, power, occupancy, plant supervision, general expense, and maintenance.

Stores is then distributed based on the amount of direct material used by the production department because stores is the primary service area that distributes raw materials to the operating departments.

Add Cost Center Overhead and Reallocations

To the cost center overhead, add its labor additives, and its share of the redistribution of both the general overhead expense and the service departments expenses, to arrive at a total allocated overhead. The total allocated overhead of $1,533,100 is the same as the sum of departmental overheads plus the labor additives.

Calculate Cost Center Rates

The rates are calculated by dividing the total adjusted overhead for each cost center by cost center direct labor to arrive at a cost center

overhead rate. This illustration of departmental overhead rate deriva-
tion is intended to reflect only one approach. The method of collecting the cost data and the basis for allocation will vary with industry
and management discretion. However, the basis procedures should
be followed consistently to provide equity among the various cost
centers of the organizations.

7

Overhead in
Government Contracts

All discussions to this point have centered around indirect cost pools as they function in a commercial or (nongovernment) manufacturing environment. But what about the multitude of firms doing business with the U.S. government? Do they record, classify, and calculate indirect rates on the same bases as those that do not contract directly with the U.S. government? Before this question can be addressed, it is necessary to provide a brief overview of the federal government's procurement practices and its authority, the basic types of government contracts awarded, and the concept of allowable costs.

PROCUREMENT PRACTICES

Each agency of the U.S. government has developed its own procurement regulations vesting the authority to bind the government in a person who is designated as the contracting officer. This individual is the only person authorized to officially bind the U.S. government on contract matters. While each agency has developed its own procurement regulations and has issued them as agency circulars, the overall authority for procurement and the regulations generally used are the Armed Services Procurement Regulations (ASPR) and the Federal Procurement Regulations (FPR). Most military or defense agencies use the procedures promulgated in ASPR, while most civilian agencies follow the FPR procedures. The two most notable exceptions are the Atomic Energy Commission (AEC) and the National Aeronautical Space Agency (NASA); they have developed their own regulations, which are in consonance with both the ASPR and the FPR. There is presently activity to combine all procurement regulations into one document.

The federal government procures products and services in two ways — by formal advertisement and by negotiation. The formal advertisement approach means that the government agency issues an Invitation for Bids (IFB) to firms known to be qualified to provide the product or service needed. The IFB contains the specifications of the needed products or services. Firms wishing to supply those products or services submit sealed bids, which are opened publicly at a specified time, and the lowest bidder is awarded the contract. There may be no further negotiation between the government and the contractor concerning price, delivery, or specifications.

In contrast to the Invitation for Bids, which allows for little or no negotiation and is issued to known qualified firms, the Request for Proposals (RFP) is advertised and available to all firms, and normally result in negotiation with several firms that are considered responsive or qualified after the proposals have been submitted and reviewed.

ALLOWABLE COSTS

The procurement regulations provide guidance to the contracting officer on all matters contained in a contract. One of the most significant influences of both the ASPR and the FPR on indirect costs is Chapter XV of the procurement regulations, entitled "Contract Cost Principles," which introduces the concept of allowable costs. Determination of allowable costs is required in order to ascertain what costs will be accepted by the government as reimbursable for performance under its contracts. Allowability of costs is determined on the basis of four tests. In order for a cost to be considered allowable it must be reasonable, it must be properly allocated, it cannot be excluded by Chapter XV of the procurement regulations, and it must be in accordance with generally accepted accounting principles. Not all costs incurred in the operation of a business should be allowed or funded through contract payments by the federal government because they are not always necessary to the operation of the product or service being provided. What types of expenses should not be included in the contract prices for products or services sold to the federal government? They can be classified as the following:

expenses that are not necessary in order to do government work;

expenses that are contrary to public policy;

expenses that are unreasonable in amount;

expenses that are part of a company's profit;

expenses that would create a double recovery of cost;

expenses that are unallowed by statute or regulation;

expenses that are unallowed in a particular contract;

expenses that are excluded by generally accepted accounting principles; and

expenses not specifically covered by the cost principles.

A few words of explanation regarding each of the above categories will clarify the government's position and reasoning.

Expenses Not Necessary in Order to do Government Work

This category contains the most cost items that are unallowed, although many of them would also be unallowed by reason of their inclusion in other categories. To understand this principle, consider the fact that any cost may be necessary to operate a business but not all costs are necessary to perform a particular contract. This is the underlying concept of this category. For example, advertising a company's product or service is necessary to create a market, but these expenses relate solely to the commercial product or service since the government seeks out vendors through Invitation for Bid (IFB) or advertises its need for services through Requests for Proposals (RFP). Therefore, the reasoning is advanced that one does not have to advertise to do business with the U.S. government. In keeping with this theory, the cost of advertising has been an unallowed cost by statute since 1971 and is not reimbursed by the government as part of the overhead expenses on contract. Likewise, writing off a bad debt or charging an appropriate reserve for a bad debt is not considered an allowable cost because the government never defaults on its contracted debts. A rule of thumb may be that, if the expense is incurred solely for the commercial portion of the business, it is not recoverable as a part of the indirect expense on government contracts.

Expenses That Are Contrary to Public Policy

The costs in this group may also be included in Category 6. The best example is gifts or entertainment provided or given to government officials, particularly those in positions to award or influence the award of government contracts.

Expenses That are Unreasonable in Amount

The most frequent items of discussion in this category are salaries and fees paid to consultants. Salaries paid to directors, officers, and managers are areas of negotiation, but a firm's position is weakened considerably if an increase follows shortly after the signing of a large government contract. The fees paid to consultants are usually reviewed in relation to the value of the service and the prevailing market condition for that service. The ASPR (paragraph 15.201.3) states that: "A cost is reasonable if it does not exceed that which would be incurred by the ordinarily prudent person in the conduct of competitive business."

Expenses That Are Part of a Company's Profit

The effects of this category could be minimized by preagreement on any items that are anticipated problems. The most notable area where such a problem may arise is in the allocation of home office expenses to geographically dispersed subsidiaries or branches. The amount to be allocated is difficult to determine. The government contends that these expenses are part of the subsidiary's or branches' profit and are recovered elsewhere by the home office.

Expenses That Would Create a Double Recovery of Cost

The underlying principle is that if costs are charged directly to government contracts that would normally be considered indirect charges, then the remaining indirect expenses should also be charged to the other work of the contractor and should be eliminated from the indirect expense pool when calculating the indirect rate applicable to the government contract.

For example, if, upon negotiating a large government contract, a firm agrees that all supplies used on the contract will become a direct charge to that contract, then the supplies remaining in the indirect cost category have to be eliminated and the indirect rate applied to that contract so that the same cost cannot be recovered twice. (See Exhibit 11.) If double recovery had occurred, the contract would have absorbed an additional $6,500 of supplies in addition to the $20,000 of direct charges.

Expenses That Are Unallowed by Statutes

The authority for unallowing expenses by statute is Chapter XV of the procurement regulations. Included in this group are the following:

bad debt
advertising costs (except for help wanted)
contributions and deductions

entertainment costs
interests
fines and penalties
excess facilities
losses on other contracts
organization costs
certain taxes

Some of these expenses are covered by other categories.

Expenses Unallowed by a Particular Contract

Some items of costs are unallowed to a particular contract by agreement between the contractor and the government at the time the contract is negotiated. An example of costs that may be excluded from recovery as a part of indirect costs could be research and development. The contracting officer, the government representative, may believe that this cost should be completely absorbed by the contractor and have language to this effect written into the contract. In many instances the contracting office will allow a portion of the costs to be recovered. A predetermined level of expenditure or a predetermined percentage of revenue for that particular cost will be negotiated before the contract is signed and that portion of the cost will be cited as recoverable in the contract. For example, experience may indicate that the firm normally spends 9 percent of revenue on marketing. The government negotiator may feel that this is higher than should be paid for by the government and will attempt to negotiate to reimburse the cost at, say, 7 percent of revenue. There are no specific guidelines that can be established to determine how much of a particular cost can be allowable. It results in a negotiated amount that appears reasonable to both parties in light of the circumstances.

Appendix B of this work reviews those elements of indirect cost that are covered by the cost principles and provides a brief description of the nature of these costs.

Expenses That Are Excluded by
Generally Accepted Accounting Principles

The accounting convention, which is presently guided by the Financial Accounting Standards Board, continuously review accounting

Exhibit 11

Double Recovery of Contract Charging

Total overhead pool	$1,500,000	(includes $45,000 of supplies not charged directly to contracts)
Total direct labor	$1,500,000	
Company overhead rate	100%	(overhead pool ÷ direct labor)

Illustration:

Contract A With Double Screening:

Direct charges (includes 20,000 of supplies charged directly to the contract)	$500,000
Direct labor	250,000
Overhead @ 100%	250,000
Total factory costs	$1,000,000

Contract A Without Double Screening:

Direct charges (includes 20,000 of supplies charged directly to contract)	$500,000
Direct labor	250,000
Overhead @ 97%	242,500
Total factory costs	$992,500

Total overhead pool:	$1,500,000
Less balance of supplies expenses	45,000
Adjusted overhead pool	1,455,000
Total direct labor	$1,500,000
Adjusted overhead rate	97% (adjusted overhead pool ÷ direct labor)

concepts and usage to determine and provide guidance in the correct and consistent recording of expenses. If an expense is included in costs that do not meet the requirements of generally accepted accounting principles, the cost may not be fully recoverable. For example, the write off through depreciation of a new piece of equipment faster than would be normally expected would require special justification for all of a cost to be allowable and therefore recoverable within a particular accounting period.

Expenses not Specifically Covered in the Cost Principles

Chapter XV of both the Armed Services Procurement Regulations (ASPR) and the Federal Procurement Regulations (FPR) outline selected items of indirect costs and establish criteria concerning their allowability. However, both regulations contain a paragraph that states that every element of indirect costs is not specifically reviewed by the cost principles. Failure to specifically identify an indirect cost in the regulation does not in itself imply that the cost is either allowable or unallowable. This will depend on the circumstances in the particular situation and, where appropriate, how similar items of cost were treated.

BASIC TYPES OF CONTRACTS

In order to understand how the concept of allowable cost works, it is important to understand the three basic and most often used types of contracts — fixed price (FP), cost-plus-fixed-fee (CPFF), and time-and-material (T&M). There are many variations of these three basic types of contracts, but a definition will suffice here.

A *fixed price contract,* also called a lump sum contract, is a contract between two parties in which the first party agrees to build a specific product or to perform a well-defined service for a fixed amount of money.

A *cost-plus-fixed-fee contract* is an agreement between two parties where the first party agrees to build a product or to provide a service for the cost incurred plus a preagreed-upon, fixed dollar amount of fee.

A *time and materials contract* is a contract in which the contractor is reimbursed for each hour of service provided at a fixed amount, which is previously agreed upon to include the labor cost, the indirect costs, and a profit. Material costs are generally recovered at cost.

The important point here is that only the cost-plus-fixed-fee contract is reimbursed for allowable costs because it is the only one of the three basic contract types in which individual elements of cost are audited to determine the amount of reimbursement.

USE OF OVERHEAD IN COST TYPE CONTRACTS

When negotiating a cost-plus-fixed-fee contract, the contractor and the contracting officer mutually agree upon a provisional overhead rate for use in determining the contract price and for interim billing during the first year of the contract. The amount reimbursed each month or each billing period is subject to adjustment on the basis of the final overhead rate developed after the year is concluded. The contractor is required to submit a summary of his indirect costs for the year, his costs used in the base for the year, and the calculation of the proposed final rates within 90 days after the fiscal year ends. The government auditors then review the company books using the guidelines and criteria for determining allowable costs. If they determine that some of the costs are not allowable, they recompute the indirect cost rates after reaching an agreement with the contractor that their findings are correct. Since their report is only advisory, if the auditor and the contractor disagree on the allowability of a particular indirect cost, the final negotiation of the rate is made between the contractor and the contracting officer. The readjusted rate, if any, is applied to the appropriate base and a credit is given to the government if the *final* rate is lower than the contractor has provisionally been reimbursed. Or, an additional billing is sent to the government if the final rate is higher than the contractor has provisionally been reimbursed and there are sufficient funds remaining in the contract to allow full recovery.

ALLOWABLE COST METHODS

There are two methods used by contractors to provide for unallowed costs. In the first method, all costs anticipated to be unallowed are recorded in accounts separate from the allowable costs. These unallowed costs are then deducted from the operating statement after all other operating costs have been considered. This means that the costs maintained by the general ledger under the indirect cost control accounts are considered allowable, and assuming that no errors in judgment are made, the allowable rates determined by the government auditors should be the same as the rates maintained by the contractor.

The second method is used more often by large contractors. It makes no distinction between allowed and unallowed costs at the time the costs are recorded, but leaves it to the government auditor to find the unallowed costs. Since the firms using this method recognize that some costs will be unallowed, they estimate the percentage of overhead that will not be recovered and reduce the rate they bid on cost-plus-fixed-fee contracts. They bid the full rate on fixed-price and time-and-material contracts since the price they receive is not subject to overhead review.

For illustrative purposes, assume that a firm projects an overhead rate of 100 percent but its experience during the past five years had indicated that an average of 2 percent of the overhead has been unallowed. These firms usually bid an overhead rate of 98 percent for CPFF work and 100 percent for fixed-price and time-and-materials contracts. They are estimating that their normal practice of incurring costs will result in 2 percent being unallowed and assume that their projected rates will then be met. If more than 2 percent is unallowed, they will still have to refund the excess cost to the government of CPFF contracts. If less than 2 percent is unallowed, they will bill additional cost on CPFF contracts to the government. The philosophy behind this approach is that it costs too much in time and money to segregate the costs and it is the government's responsibility to find the unallowed costs.

BID AND PROPOSAL (B&P) COSTS

Earlier it was explained that the two pricing procurement regulations used by the military and the civilian agencies were the Armed Services Procurement Regulations and the Federal Procurements Regulations, respectively. A review of the regulations reveals that they are very much alike. However, in the case of indirect cost, they differ in one major respect.

Both regulations define bidding cost as those costs incurred in preparing proposals to the government. They state further that the proposal costs of both successful and unsuccessful proposals are considered allowable costs. The difference between the procurement regulations regarding proposal cost is that the FPR does not state the indirect pool with which the expense is associated (overhead or general and administrative); it is left to the discretion of management. On the other hand, the ASPR states as a general rule that bid and proposal costs shall be allocated to contracts on the same basis as general and administrative expenses, unless this results in an inequitable cost allocation. In such a case, the contracting office can approve a different basis.

When the change in ASPR occurred in 1971, the Department of Defense issued a circular that outlined a formula for transferring the B&P overhead costs to G&A. If a firm performing a Defense Department contract had its B&P cost accumulated in overhead, then it must exclude from overhead all B&P costs. It then divides the B&P costs into two parts — labor and other direct costs. The labor is added to the regular direct labor base and forms a new base for overhead rate calculation. The new base is divided into the net overhead (the overhead without any B&P costs) to obtain an adjusted overhead rate. The new adjusted overhead rate is then applied to the B&P labor. The total of B&P labor, the applied overhead, and the balance of the other direct B&P costs are added to the G&A expense. The G&A base is then adjusted for the newly calculated B&P cost, which is transferred to G&A.

The effects on the overhead and G&A rate can be significant, as can be seen in Exhibit 12. The total cost has not changed but it has been reconstituted to reflect the ASPR change. The application of both rates is very difficult, and it is, therefore, advisable to adopt either one method or the other but not both.

Exhibit 12

B&P Cost From Overhead to G&A

Cost with B&P in Overhead

Overhead

Indirect labor—nonsales	$ 500,000
Direct costs—nonsales	750,000
Indirect labor—sales	300,000
Direct costs—sales	300,000
Total overhead	$1,850,000
Direct labor	$1,850,000
Overhead rate (Total overhead ÷ direct labor)	100%

G&A

Total indirect labor	$ 375,000
Direct costs	573,000
Total G&A expense	$ 948,000

G&A Base

Direct labor	$1,850,000
Overhead	1,850,000
Contract direct charges	4,200,000
Total G&A base	$7,900,000
G&A rate (G&A expense ÷ G&A base)	12%

Cost with B&P transferred to G&A

Total overhead		$1,850,000
Less: B&P labor	$300,000	
non B&P costs	300,000	600,000
Adjusted overhead cost		$1,250,000
Direct labor		$1,850,000
Add: B&P labor		300,000
Adjusted direct labor base		$2,150,000
Adjusted overhead rate (Adjusted overhead cost ÷		58.14%
adjusted direct labor base)		
G&A costs		$ 948,000
Add: B&P labor	$300,000	
Adjusted overhead		
@ 58.14%	174,420	
B&P nonlabor	300,000	774,420
Adjusted G&A cost		$1,722,420
G&A base		$7,900,000
Less cost transferred to G&A*		−774,420
Adjusted G&A base		$7,125,580
Adjusted G&A rate (G&A cost ÷ G&A base)		23.69%

*Cost transferred	
B&P labor	$300,000
Adjusted B&P overhead	174,420
Nonlabor B&P costs	300,000
	$774,420

8

Other Costing Methods

The use of overhead, selling, and general and administrative rates is the standard approach employed by most firms. This chapter will deal with a discussion of how rates can be used to gain a competitive advantage and of the special rates used by firms to provide more precise costing.

If the primary difference between overhead, selling, and general and administrative expenses is that overhead is associated with producing a product and can be capitalized into inventory, while selling and administrative costs must be written off in the period in which they were incurred, then what is the advantage of having more than one overhead rate in a service company where there is no inventorial product? Since there is no inventory, why not just summarize all costs in one control account and apply one rate? Certainly, having more than one overhead control account, determining a proper classification of expenses according to types of indirect pools, determining more than one equitable base, and applying more than one overhead rate is more costly and time-consuming.

In the commercial and retail fields, except where a custom service is provided, the distinction is not important. The customer is interested only in the total price that he is charged and not in a breakdown of the costs within that price. However, when the firm must compete on a detailed cost basis with other service firms, the breakdown of the cost becomes important. When the breakdown of cost is reviewed, the direct cost, labor, and materials are determinable, so the focal point of discussion usually becomes the rate of indirect expenses that the firm is applying. Many buyers develop preset guidelines that establish ceilings on indirect expense rates. Anything higher than the rate they consider too high. This rate varies from buyer to buyer.

In order to counteract this bias, many service firms develop separate rates. For example, suppose it is known that a buyer considers any rate higher than 100 percent to be high, and a firm's rates for the next year are projected at 100 percent. Because of keen competition, the firm desires to present its best position and decides to begin bidding an overhead rate and a G&A rate. This revision of the firm's cost accounting system leads to rates of 75 percent for overhead and 8.3 percent for G&A. As can be seen below, the splitting of the cost does not change the total overhead costs, but it does present a more cosmetically favorable rate to the buyer.

Projected Costs		Cost with One Rate		Cost with Two Rates
Material		$1,500,000		$1,500,000
Direct labor		1,200,000		1,200,000
Overhead	@ 100%	1,200,000	@ 75%	900,000
Costs		$3,900,000		$3,600,000
G&A	@ 0%		@ 8.3%	300,000
Total cost		$3,900,000		$3,900,000

Less direct cost:

Material:	1,500,000		
Direct labor:	1,200,000	−2,700,000	−2,700,000
Total indirect costs		$1,200,000	$1,200,000

To better understand this relationship, consider the following question: Is a rate of 105 percent of direct labor higher or lower than a rate of 90 percent for overhead based on direct labor plus 10 percent for G&A based on total cost input (exclusive of G&A costs)?

Based on the information provided so far, a decision cannot be made. The determination cannot be made until the nonlabor direct costs are known. A firm using a G&A rate quickly finds that the amount of direct or prime cost greatly affects the G&A rate. A review of Exhibit 8 clearly indicates that, in this example, the 105 percent rate is lower than the 90 percent overhead plus the 10 percent G&A. However, reducing the amount of nonlabor direct costs in Exhibit 9 reflects the sensitivity of the G&A rate to direct costs and indicates that 105 percent overhead in this case is higher than a 90 percent overhead plus a 10 percent G&A rate. While this is very subtle and much analysis is not needed to discount the advantages, the cost splitting simply provides a good first impression for the rates.

The implication of this discussion is not that there is anything improper or deceptive in splitting the costs into two or more rates. Nor is it improper for the firm to make a decision to have more than one rate. In fact, this is perfectly proper accounting. The example shown above merely illustrates that the quotable rates must be analyzed in order to evaluate the real indirect rates effect. A general rule to follow is that, the more the rates are additive to other accumulated costs, the higher the actual indirect costs become.

Another method that has gained popularity in recent years is the splitting of the overhead rate into two parts — fringe benefits and other overhead. The fringe benefit portion of overhead is closely associated with labor. Firms have begun to realize that the total employees' cost is much more than the salaries they are paid, that the benefits that the employees receive are a real part of their compensation. Therefore, a total compensation concept has developed by which benefits are segregated from other overhead and are included in employee compensation.

Two approaches are generally used. The first is really as much cosmetic as it is real. In this approach, the total of fringe benefits is segregated from the overhead and is divided by the total salaries to calculate a fringe benefit rate. The rate calculated is then applied to the direct labor and the product that results is added to the direct labor base in order to calculate a total compensation base. The new loaded base is divided into the remaining overhead to derive an overhead rate based on total compensation.

For example, a firm projects direct labor for the year of $500,000 and a total overhead of $500,000, or an overhead rate of 100 percent and, through separate analysis, determines a fringe rate of 20 percent. Therefore, included in the $500,000 of overhead expenses is $100,000 of fringe benefits that relate to the direct labor. The direct labor base is increased by this amount and the overhead expenses are reduced by this amount. The adjusted direct labor (direct labor plus the associated fringe) is divided into the adjusted overhead (overhead less fringe associated with direct labor) to calculate a new overhead rate of 66.7 percent as shown below:

	Direct Labor	*Overhead*	
Total	$500,000	$500,000	100.0%
Fringe benefits	100,000	(100,000)	
Adjusted balances	$600,000	$400,000	66.7%
Overrun of fringe rate (2% x 500,000)		10,000	
Adjusted balances for overrun	$600,000	$410,000	68.3%

It is assumed in this example that the overrun for labor benefits included in the overhead were absorbed within the $400,000 estimate. As stated earlier, this system more nearly relates to the concept of total compensation. In practice, when this system is used, a breakdown of the fringe benefits included in labor is almost always requested in any cost breakdown. But fringe benefits, unless they are unusually out of line, are not normally a matter for negotiation.

When many of the manufacturing firms producing consumer products expanded into the government's heavy arms and missile business, they soon realized that their costs and their investment in voluminous raw materials and subassemblies increased significantly.

In order to handle this production, an increase in the size of the staffs, or purchasing and related processing, raw material stores, subassembly stores, and parts inventory, was needed. To more precisely calculate costs and to segregate the costs from the commercial products, it was decided in many firms to collect these costs in a burden center and to attach them to material processing through a materials handling rate. This cost was passed on to the proper users of the system as a special overhead rate, which also reduced the normal overhead rate.

A major manufacturer of missile systems discovered that it was spending hundreds of thousands of dollars each year on electronic productive supplies. These diodes, capacitors, resistors, etc., were too inexpensive individually to cost to the projects. Yet collectively they were very expensive if they were included in overhead. A review of the use of these supplies indicated that they were predominantly used during the assembly phase of manufacturing. Further analysis revealed that, for each hour of assembly work, a reasonably uniform dollar value of the supplies was used. It was decided to buy those items and to place their cost in a special inventory account. For each hour of assembly work performed on a project, a fixed dollar amount of electronic productive supplies was charged. A physical inventory was taken at the end of each year and the difference was written off to overhead.

Firms that operate their own computers sometimes establish a special overhead account to collect all of their operating costs. The debit (left) side of the account collects the costs of the computer, the staff used to operate the computer, and all related supplies. The credit (right) side of the account is used to internally bill the users. Generally, the billing is at a markup rate to cover the cost of the computer tape library maintenance and the cost of developing additional programs. In some instances, the corporate services of accounting and corporate management data processing are also covered by the surplus billing.

Another billing method is to convert service group expenses to direct costs by establishing billing rates for these services. The concept is the same as the computer system above; the costs are collected and billed to the users at a rate that will break even over the accounting fiscal year.

The method used to bill can vary, but it must be equitable and reasonable to the user. This approach is particularly effective in distributing as direct costs graphic services, typing services, and printing, xeroxing, and editing services. It can be used for almost any cost where the service to a particular cost objective is identifiable and measurable, and where it is easier to collect the cost back from the customer as a direct charge. It should not be done until a complete analysis of the cost and the effect of the charge have been made because, while overhead is being reduced by transferring some of the overhead cost to direct cost, adverse effects on the base used for rate calculation may also be taking place.

For example, assume that a firm desires to transfer the graphics department to a direct charge center and management is presented with the following data:

Total company direct labor	$4,000,000
Total company overhead	$5,000,000
Graphics portion of direct labor	$ 60,000
Graphics contribution to overhead	$ 30,000
Company overhead rate	125%

If, based on the above information, management decides to establish graphics as a direct center, it would recover the $90,000 as direct charges. But its overhead rate would increase to 138 percent because graphics had been contributing more to the original base of direct labor and less to overhead than the average of other departments in the company.

	Direct Labor	Overhead	Rate
Total	$4,000,000	$5,000,000	125%
Less graphics	(60,000)	(30,000)	
Adjusted total	$3,940,000	$4,970,000	138.2%

As this example shows, if it is determined that the department under consideration had an overhead rate calculated independently that was less than the company rate, then if all other things are equal as well, it is not normally justifiable to establish the department as a direct cost center.

As shown above, it is important to understand that both the direct and indirect costs of the section under consideration must be removed from total costs before calculating a new overhead rate. The base used previously does not have to be the base for the new direct cost center. In the above illustration, direct labor was the base used previously, but the size of drawings or illustrations may be the new base for distributing cost in the new direct cost center. Some common bases used for direct cost centers are the following:

Direct Cost Centers	*Bases*
Graphics	Size of drawing or illustration
Printing	Number of images
Xerox	Number of images
Typing	Number of pages; unit rate per hour
Editing	Number of pages; unit rate per hour

The direct cost center can be an effective tool if it is used properly and run efficiently.

In the 1930s, a new variation of the cost accounting system was introduced. It was called direct costing.

Absorption costing allocates all overhead expenses to product costs. In direct costing, only the variable costs are allocated to product costs.* Those who advocate direct costing believe that fixed costs go beyond the immediate controls of the department or the operating manager and therefore should not be their responsibility but should be considered as period charges. As indicated earlier, variable overhead expenses vary with changes in production. However, there is no fine line that distinguishes one cost as fixed and another as variable. In many ways, it is a management decision whether a cost is considered fixed or variable. As previously indicated, most costs are semivariable, having characteristics of both. Therefore, it is very difficult to make a distinction. For this reason, the distinction between fixed and variable is very arbitrary and is governed by the practical considerations of the particular situation. The primary objection to direct costing is that corporate manage-

---

*Fixed overhead expenses are charged as period costs and not as product costs.

ment must be alert at all times in reviewing the level of fixed costs in order to assure that the revenue volume is sufficient to at least make the operation break even. While this is the primary objection to the direct costing method, it is also one of its strengths: because the fixed and variable costs are segregated in the system, the break-even analysis is done with very little effort.

The purpose of discussing all of these overhead variations is to demonstrate the variety, ease, and flexibility within the accounting structure that enable better costing and provide management with more useful operating knowledge. The following questions are the criteria used for deciding to change an overhead structure:

Does the new system provide a competitive advantage?

Does the new structure provide better costing data?

Is the new structure easier to use?

Is the new system equitable?

If the answers to the above questions are all "yes," then it may be to the firm's advantage to consider making an accounting system change.

None of the accounting overhead variations presented above is designed to deceive, nor is any of them illegal or unethical. They are simply legitimate, proven systems used by management to obtain better cost information.

Part 1: Self-evaluation Exercises

The following questions and problems are designed to help you evaluate how well you retained and understood the information in each chapter. The author has provided answers to the questions and problems in Part 2 of this appendix. There are no passing or failing mark to this exercise; you must personally determine how well you understood the chapter. If you get a different answer or do not understand the answer, reread the chapter so that you have a clearer understanding of the concept.

Chapter 1

1-1 What criteria are used to determine if a labor cost is charged direct or indirect?

1-2 Which classifications of cost are associated with production and which are associated with commercial costs?

1-3 Classify as direct or indirect the following items used in a breakfast food plant:

sugar	barley
paper boxes	oats
paper box liners	gas for cooking
cinnamon	peanuts
soap for lavatories	glue for sealing boxes

1-4 Define the following terms:

cost objectives	direct charges
direct labor	premium labor
other direct charges	

Chapter 2

2-1 Explain the differences in accounting theory of overhead, selling, and general and administrative expenses.

2-2 The following information is available on product number 4382:

Direct Labor Cost	Cost	Hours
Week of Nov. 8	$8,000	2,000
Week of Nov. 15	$9,000	2,250
Week of Nov. 22	$8,500	2,125
Week of Nov. 29	$8,700	2,175

Direct Material Costs

Material purchased directly for job	$21,352
Material issued from stores	7,750
Material returned to stores	250

Manufacturing Overhead

Applied at the rate of $ .80 per direct labor hours.

Other Direct Charges

Electronic supplies equals 7% of store's material costs used.

General and Administrative Expenses

To be charged at the rate of 10% of total cost (before G & A).

Unit Production

During November, 6,700 units of product 4382 were produced.

Required:

2-2a Calculate the total amount of costs placed in inventory for product 4382.

2-2b What was the unit cost for product 4382 during the month of November?

2-3 You are presented with the following operating statement for the Zeno Company. Would you adjust the statement or accept it as presented?

Revenue		$1,200,000
Cost of Goods Sold		
Beginning inventory (5,000 units @ $100)		$500,000
Material purchased during year	$300,000	
Direct labor	450,000	
Overhead expense	300,000	
Selling expense	90,000	
G & A expense	100,000	
Total current year cost (10,000 units)		1,240,000
Total cost in inventory (15,000 @ $115)		$1,740,000
Less inventory at year end (6,000 @ $116)		696,000
Cost of goods sold		−1,044,000
Operating profit		$ 156,000

Chapter 3

3-1 Assign the following expenses to one of the three basic classifications (overhead, selling, and general and administrative):

accounting labor   janitorial labor
executive labor   legal services
maintenance labor   outside service repair
office supplies   operating supplies
telephone   power, heat, & water
postage   travel
advertising   property taxes
rent — building   depreciation
relocation expenses   help wanted advertising

3-2 Regroup the following partial list of expenses according to the
     purpose of the expense:

     1. labor for preparing a proposal
     2. travel for corporate general business
     3. xeroxing for a sole-source bid
     4. conference fees
     5. telephone costs for president's office
     6. heat, light, power
     7. legal expenses related to specific contract problem
     8. labor of maintenance staff
     9. graphics labor for proposal
     10. travel to conference
     11. help wanted advertisement
     12. labor for personnel department
     13. travel of employee during relocation
     14. consultant for contract
     15. xerox for president's office

3-3 Which is more important to know — the total cost by type of
     expense or by purpose of expense?

4-1 The Xcel Company's records reflect the following informa-
     tion:

Month	Overhead Applied	Overhead Actual
January	$50,000	$55,000
February	55,000	57,000
March	60,000	57,000
April	57,000	58,000

May	68,000	58,000
June	62,000	59,000
July	58,000	67,000
August	55,000	53,000
September	50,000	55,000
October	47,000	44,000
November	48,000	44,000
December	52,000	57,000

Required:

4-1 Compute the cumulative balance that is either over- or under-applied each month.

4-2 Using T accounts, reflect the results of the following information for the actual overhead account, the applied overhead account, and the cost of goods sold at year-end, May 31, and prepare entries for year-end.

The overhead applied at December 31 was $1,575,000. For the period January through May, it was $250,000, $255,000, $262,000, $271,000, and $269,000, respectively.

The actual expense for overhead at December 31 was $1,575,000, and for the period January through May it was $252,000, $271,000, $268,000, $269,000, and $265,000, respectively.

4-3 The Best Company does not use an applied overhead rate. Instead it allocates the actual overhead expenses incurred each month to jobs based on the actual labor hours used for that month. Below are the actual labor hours and the actual overhead expenses for the last three (3) months.

	January	February	March
Actual overhead	$120,000	$100,000	$112,000
Actual labor hours	25,000	20,000	28,000

During the three-month period, one customer sent an identical order each month for the production of 2,000 units, each requiring direct labor of 2,000 hours at an average of $7.00 per hour and material of $8,000.

Required:

4-3a What was the total cost and the unit cost for the job in each of the three months?

4-3b What recommendations do you have regarding the method of allocating overhead?

Chapter 5

5-1 Define: Fixed, variable, and semivariable expenses.

5-2 The Refuss Company, as part of its procedure of estimating expenses, classifies all expenses as being either fixed or variable. However, in order to arrive at such a classification, it is necessary to analyze each semivariable expense to determine what part of the expense is fixed and to lessen the degree of variability of the remaining portion. As part of the analysis, the expense for supervision is being studied. You are called on to assist in the analysis, and you discover that the company's backlog indicates a 25% growth in revenues with a corresponding growth required in supervision. A review of the previous year's expenses reveals the following information:

	Revenue	Supervision Cost
	(in thousands)	
January	$1,000	150
February	1,200	170
March	1,800	230
April	1,500	200
May	1,500	200
June	2,200	270
July	2,000	250
August	2,100	260
September	2,500	300
October	2,800	330
November	3,000	350
December	3,500	400

Required:

Compute the degree of variability of the supervision expense, as well as the fixed part of the expense, using the high-low method.

5-3 The Alcorn Company estimates its overhead expense for the next period at $600,000. It is estimated that 25,000 units will be produced at a material cost of $125,000. Production will require 175,000 hours at an estimated wage cost of $525,000. The machine will run about 50,000 hours.

Required:

From the information provided, determine the overhead expense rate that may be used in applying overhead expenses to production on each of the following bases:

a. unit of production
b. material cost basis
c. direct labor cost basis
d. direct labor hours basis
e. machine hours basis

Chapter 6

6-1 The Rencel Company estimated the following for the year:

| | Department | | | Service |
	1	2	3	X
Floor space (sq. ft.)	1,500	4,500	3,000	1,000
Value of machinery	$10,000	$10,000	$20,000	$10,000
Horsepower hours	2,500	2,500	5,000	2,000
Number of employees ·	15	25	25	10
Indirect material cost	$ 1,250	$ 1,150	$ 500	$ 500
Direct labor cost	$25,000	$45,000	$30,000	—
Indirect labor cost	$ 2,000	$ 1,500	$ 1,500	$10,000

Estimated general manufacturing expenses not listed above were:

Rent	$ 2,000
Repairs to building	$10,000
Depreciation of machinery	5% of Investment
Superintendent	$ 7,500
Power	$ 3,600
Insurance on machinery	$ 1,000

Service Department X was distributed as follows:

Department 1 — 1/7
Department 2 — 4/7
Department 3 — 2/7

Required:

Determine the manufacturing expense rate for each producing department on the basis of direct labor cost.

6-2 The Systplan Consulting firm uses only one rate for applying overhead, but believes that it would have better cost data and be more competitive if it used departmental rates. The company has hired you to review its data and determine the best method of allocating cost so that departmental rates can be used.

The following information is available: the company has five (5) operating departments and a maintenance department, with one general overhead account to collect company-wide overhead expenses. All of the corporate support departments, such as accounting, legal, etc., are considered general and administrative expenses and are not in the overhead rate.

Departments: Economics, Transportation, Environment, Urban Planning, Health

	Direct Labor
Economics	$ 262,868
Transportation	169,323
Environment	177,961
Urban Planning	630,376
Health	108,668
Total	$1,349,196

Overhead charged directly to operating departments:

	Total	Indirect Labor	Indirect Nonlabor
Economics	$109,554	$16,433	$ 93,121
Transportation	142,725	21,409	121,316
Environment	116,720	11,672	105,048
Urban Planning	132,670	26,534	106,136
Health	101,136	11,125	90,011

Expense in general overhead accounts:

Personnel placement and relocation expenses	$ 64,914
Depreciation expenses	72,273
Telephone expenses	62,421
Office supplies	4,568
Maintenance	46,805
Rent and related expenses	185,961
Other general expenses	130,937
Total general overhead expense	$567,879

	Square Footage	Number of Employees	Number of Phones	Value of Equipment
Economics	10,000	15	18	$15,000
Transportation	12,000	13	20	13,000
Environment	9,000	10	15	10,000
Urban Planning	25,000	40	50	50,000
Health	14,000	15	15	15,000

Required:

6-2a Calculate the departmental overhead rate.

6-3 An evaluation of the Zerxes Company reveals:

Direct Labor:

Department A	$20,000
Department B	$40,000
Department C	$30,000

The following departmental expenses were incurred during the year:

| | Service Departments | | |
| | | Machine | |
	Storeroom	Shop	Engineering
Supervision	$3,600	$ 4,000	$8,000
Indirect labor	4,400	12,000	7,000
Insurance	150	300	250
Machinery repairs	—	1,780	400
Depreciation of machines	—	1,680	500
Supplies	530	600	1,250

| | Production Department | | |
	A	B	C
Supervision	$6,000	$8,000	$ 7,000
Indirect labor	3,000	3,000	8,000
Insurance	850	940	1,250
Machinery repairs	900	1,200	1,600
Depreciation of machines	6,000	8,000	10,000
Supplies	2,410	2,940	2,750

The storeroom analyzed the number of requisitions handled during the year:

Department	Number of Requisitions
Machine shop	2,800
Engineering	700
Department A	9,800
Department B	6,300
Department C	15,400

The machine shop has analyzed the amount of time spent on work for other departments as follows:

Department	Time Spent (hours)
Engineering	1,400
Department A	2,800
Department B	4,200
Department C	5,600

The fixed charges for real estate taxes, building depreciation, heat, repairs, and insurance total $20,000. The building has 150,000 square feet, divided as follows:

Department	Square Footage Occupied
Department A	24,000
Department B	24,000
Department C	72,000
Store	6,000
Machine Shop	14,000
Engineering	10,000

Required:

6-3a Calculate the overhead rates for the production departments.

Chapter 7

7-1 Explain the concept of allowable cost.

7-2 You are a government auditor and the ZD Corporation has presented the following costs for your review. The ZD Corporation does all defense department work under the authority of the Armed Services Procurement Regulations. If we assume that all the costs are allowable, would you accept the rates as submitted? If not, what rates would you accept?

Plant Overhead Costs

Indirect shop labor	$ 180,900
Proposal labor	175,900
Shop supervision labor	50,300
Repair & maintenance — machinery	40,600
Power, heat, & light	80,700
Freight in	20,000
Plant travel	13,000
Plant property taxes	95,000
Plant machinery & furniture depreciation	52,000
Plant rent	250,000
Proposal nonlabor costs	192,300
Sundry	106,100
Total plant overhead costs	$1,256,800
Total direct labor	$1,256,800
Plant overhead rate	100%

G&A Costs

Supervision labor	$ 50,000
Administrative & clerical labor	175,000
Executive labor	50,000
Telephone	52,000
Postage	4,000
Office rent	15,000
Corporate travel	8,000
Sundry	25,100
Total G&A	$ 379,100
G&A base	$3,791,000
G&A rate	10.00%

Chapter 8

8-1 Why is it important to know the direct contract cost before a determination can be made of which of the following is actually the highest total cost: 100% overhead versus 73% overhead and 10% G&A?

8-2   Which is the higher overhead, a composite overhead rate of
      105% on direct labor, or a fringe rate of 28% calculated as a
      percentage of total payroll and an overhead rate of 62% on
      total compensation? Total compensation is defined as direct
      labor plus related fringes.

8-3   You are hired as a consultant to help management decide if
      they should establish the computer and the programming staff
      as a direct charge center. Presently the computer is charged to
      contracts at cost, and the staff programmers charge their time
      to contracts and have full overhead applied. You are provided
      the following information — what would be your decision?

Total direct labor	$1,500,000
Total overhead	$1,500,000
Computer staff direct labor (included in base above)	$ 125,000
Computer staff overhead labor (included in overhead above)	$ 75,000
Computer charges to contract	$1,000,000
Computer hours charged to contract	6,000
Direct contract charges (exclusive of computer contract charges)	$4,000,000
G & A expense	$ 720,000

APPENDIX A

Part 2: Answers to Self-evaluation Exercises

Chapter 1

1-1 The criteria used to determine whether a labor cost is charged direct or indirect are: if the labor costs are specifically incurred for the benefit of a cost objective and the costs are of a sufficient amount to merit identification and measurement, then the cost should be charged direct. The measurability of the cost is usually related to the smallest element of time used for payroll purposes. In a service industry, nothing less than an hour may be charged, whereas a production shop may use smaller units of an hour.

1-2 The classification of cost included in production costs are direct material, direct production labor, other direct charges, and the overhead related to production. Selling expenses and general and administrative expenses are considered commercial costs and are not included in the production costs.

1-3   *Direct Costs*   *Indirect Costs*

    sugar   paper box liners

    paper boxes   cinnamon

    barley   soap for lavatories

    oats   gas for cooking

    peanuts   glue for sealing boxes

1-4   Cost Objective — Any function for which cost is accumulated.

    Direct Labor — Wages incurred for the benefit of a particular product or client service and traceable to that product or client service.

    Other Direct Charges — A hybrid cost that has many properties of direct materials in that it is incurred for the benefit of a particular cost objective, can be measured, and whose cost warrants cost accumulation although it may not have all of the physical properties of material.

    Direct Charges — Any cost (material, labor, or other direct charges) that is incurred for a specific cost objective.

    Premium Labor — That portion of the wage that is paid for work performed beyond the regular work day or work week.

2-1   Overhead — These indirect expenses are specifically related to producing a product or providing a service. The costs accumulated in this indirect pool can be capitalized (included) in inventory and are included as a part of the unit costs.

    Selling — These indirect costs relate to the planning and managing of the sales effort and the cost of distributing the product or service. These costs cannot be included in inventory and must be written off in the accounting period incurred.

    General and Administrative Expenses — These indirect expenses relate to the cost incurred in the general business operation of the firm. These expenses cannot be included in inventory and must be written off in the accounting period in which they were incurred.

2-2a Direct Labor $34,200
     Material — Purchased   21,352
     Net Material — Stores   7,500
     Other direct charges   525
     Manufacturing overhead
     ($ .80 x 8,550 hours)   6,840
       Total inventorial costs $70,417

2-2b $\dfrac{\text{Total inventorial costs}}{\text{units produced}} = \dfrac{\$70,417}{6,700} = \$10.51$ unit cost

2-3   Revenue $1,200,000

     Cost of Goods Sold

       Beginning inventory
         (5,000 units @ $100) $ 500,000

       Material purchased
         during year $300,000
       Direct labor   450,000
       Overhead expense   300,000

       Total current year
         cost (10,000 units)   1,050,000

       Total cost in inven-
         tory (5,000 units @
         $100 & 10,000 units
         @ $105) $1,550,000

       Ending inventory
         (6,000 units @ $105)   630,000

        Cost of goods sold   920,000

        Gross profit $280,000

      Less selling expense $ 90,000

      Less G&A expense   100,000

                               190,000

        Operating Profit $ 90,000

The way the Zeno Company statement was originally presented, $66,000 of selling and general and administrative expenses were included in the year-end inventory.

3-1		
Accounting labor	G & A
Executive labor	G & A
Maintenance labor	Overhead
Office supplies*	G & A
Telephone*	G & A
Postage*	G & A
Advertising	Selling
Rent — building	Overhead
Relocation expenses	G & A
Janitorial labor	Overhead
Legal service	G & A
Outside service repaid	Overhead
Operating supplies	Overhead
Power, heat, & water	Overhead
Travel*	G & A
Property taxes	Overhead
Depreciation	Overhead
Help wanted advertising	G & A

3-2 Proposal Preparation
  1. labor for preparing proposal
  3. xeroxing for a sole-source proposal
  9. graphics labor for a proposal

---

*These expenses can be allocated to overhead and selling also if the management of the firm desires a more equitable distribution of costs.

General Corporate Business
2. travel for corporate general business
5. telephone costs for president's office
15. xerox for president's office

Conference Expense
4. conference fees
10. travel to conference

Occupancy Expenses
6. heat, light, and power
8. labor for maintenance staff

Direct Contract Costs (ODC)
7. legal expense related to specific contract problem
14. consultant for contract

Personnel and Placement Costs
11. help wanted advertisement
12. labor for personnel department
13. travel of employee during relocation

3-3 There is no single answer to this question. It depends on the
     needs of management. The management of a heavy manufactur-
     ing firm with one or two products may find that the more
     traditional expense classified by type is more useful because
     there would be little variance from year to year as to the
     purpose of the expense. The variation that would occur each
     year is the change in the amount within the same type of
     expense. A service organization with changing clients may find
     it necessary to know why the costs are being incurred in order
     to control the costs. Management must make its own decision
     based on the need for information, the need to control costs,
     the stability of costs from year to year, and the expense of
     maintaining costs by either method.

4-1

Month	Overhead Applied	Cumulative Overhead Applied	Overhead Actual	Cumulative Overhead Actual	Over-Under Applied
January	$50,000	$ 50,000	$55,000	$55,000	$5,000
February	55,000	105,000	57,000	112,000	7,000
March	60,000	165,000	57,000	169,000	4,000
April	57,000	222,000	58,000	227,000	5,000
May	68,000	290,000	58,000	285,000	(5,000)
June	62,000	352,000	59,000	344,000	(8,000)
July	58,000	410,000	67,000	411,000	1,000
August	55,000	465,000	53,000	464,000	(1,000)
September	50,000	515,000	55,000	519,000	4,000
October	47,000	562,000	44,000	563,000	1,000
November	48,000	610,000	44,000	607,000	(3,000)
December	52,000	662,000	57,000	664,000	2,000

4-2

Overhead Actual

Thru	Dec. 31	$1,575,000		May 31	$2,882,000
	Jan. 31	252,000			
	Feb. 28	271,000			
	Mar. 31	268,000			
	Apr. 30	269,000			
	May 31	265,000		May 31	18,000
		$2,900,000			$2,900,000

Overhead Applied

May 31	$2,882,000		Thru	Dec. 31	$1,575,000
				Jan. 31	250,000
				Feb. 28	255,000
				Mar. 31	262,000
				Apr. 30	271,000
				May 31	269,000
	$2,882,000				$2,882,000

Cost of Goods Sold

Thru	Dec. 31	$1,575,000
	Jan. 31	250,000
	Feb. 28	255,000
	Mar. 31	262,000
	Apr. 30	271,000
	May 31	269,000
		$2,882,000
	May 31	18,000
		$2,900,000

4-3a

	January	February	March
Material	$ 8,000	$ 8,000	$ 8,000
Labor	14,000	14,000	14,000
Overhead	9,600	10,000	8,000
Total costs	$31,600	$32,000	$30,000
Units produced	2,000	2,000	2,000
Unit cost	$ 15.80	$ 16.00	$ 15.00

4-3b Based on only the information provided, you might recommend a yearly or at least a cumulative rate so that the unit cost would be more stable.

5-1   Fixed Expense — A cost that does not vary with production.

Variable Expense — A cost that changes in size in direct proportion to a change in production volume.

Semivariable Expense — A cost that varies in size with production but not in direct proportion to the change in the size of production.

5-2

	Revenue	Change	Supervision Cost	Change
January	$1,000,000		$150,000	—
February	1,200,000	$200,000	170,000	$20,000
April	1,500,000	300,000	200,000	30,000
May	1,500,000	—	200,000	—

	Revenue	Change	Supervision Cost	Change
March	$1,800,000	$ 300,000	$230,000	$ 30,000
July	2,000,000	200,000	250,000	20,000
August	2,100,000	100,000	260,000	10,000
June	2,200,000	100,000	270,000	10,000
September	2,500,000	300,000	300,000	30,000
October	2,800,000	300,000	330,000	30,000
November	3,000,000	200,000	350,000	20,000
December	3,500,000	500,000	400,000	50,000
		$2,500,000		$250,000

$$\frac{250,000}{\$2,500,000} = .10 \text{ per unit}$$

Revenue	$ .10 Variable Cost of Supervison per Unit	Total Supervision Cost	Fixed Cost
$1,000,000	$100,000	$150,000	$50,000
1,200,000	120,000	170,000	50,000
1,500,000	150,000	200,000	50,000
1,500,000	150,000	200,000	50,000
1,800,000	180,000	230,000	50,000
2,000,000	200,000	250,000	50,000
2,100,000	210,000	260,000	50,000
2,200,000	220,000	270,000	50,000
2,500,000	250,000	300,000	50,000
2,800,000	280,000	330,000	50,000
3,000,000	300,000	350,000	50,000
3,500,000	350,000	400,000	50,000

5-3   a) Unit of Production

$$\frac{\$600,000}{25,000} = \$24.00 \text{ per unit}$$

b) Material Cost Basis

$$\frac{\$600,000}{\$125,000} = \$4.80 \text{ per direct material dollar}$$

c) Direct Labor Cost Basis

$$\frac{\$600,000}{\$525,000} = \$1.1429 \text{ per labor dollar}$$

d) Direct Labor Hour Basis

$$\frac{\$600,000}{175,000} = \$3.4286 \text{ per labor hour}$$

e) Machine Hour Basis

$$\frac{\$600,000}{50,000} = \$12.00 \text{ per machine hour}$$

6-1

Rencel Company
Department Overhead Rates

Department	Direct labor	Departmental overhead	Superintendent costs	Occupancy costs	Power	Machinery costs	Service department	Total allocated overhead	Allocated overhead rate
Number 1	$ 25,000	$ 3,250	$1,500	$ 1,800	$ 750	$ 700	$ 2,000	$10,000	40.00%
Number 2	45,000	2,650	2,500	5,400	750	700	8,000	20,000	44.44%
Number 3	30,000	2,000	2,500	3,600	1,500	1,400	4,000	15,000	50.00%
Service X		10,500	1,000	1,200	600	700	(14,000)	–	
General expense		26,600	(7,500)	(12,000)	(3,600)	(3,500)	–0–	–	
	$100,000	$45,000	–0–	–0–	–0–	–0–	–0–	$45,000	45.00%
Basis for allocation			Number of people served	Floor space	Horsepower	Machinery value	Departments served		

6-2

SYSTPLAN
Departmental Overhead Rate Calculation

Departments	Direct labor	Departmental overhead	Occupancy expense	Telephone expense	Depreciation expense	People-related expenses	Other general expenses	Total allocated overhead	Allocated overhead rate
Economics	$ 262,868	$ 109,554	$ 33,252	$ 9,522	$10,525	$11,205	$ 25,460	$ 199,518	75.90%
Transportation	169,323	142,725	39,902	10,580	9,122	9,711	17,386	229,426	135.50%
Environment	177,961	116,720	29,927	7,935	7,017	7,470	17,286	186,355	104.72%
Urban planning	630,376	132,670	83,131	26,449	35,084	29,891	59,882	367,107	58.24%
Health	108,668	101,136	46,554	7,935	10,525	11,205	10,923	188,278	173.26%
General overhead		567,879	(232,766)	(62,421)	(72,273)	(69,482)	(130,937)		
	$1,349,196	$1,170,684	–0–	–0–	–0–	–0–	–0–	$1,170,684	86.77%
Basis of allocation			Square footage	Number of telephone	Value of equipment	Number of people	Total departmental labor		

6-3

Department	Direct labor	Departmental overhead	General expenses	Storeroom	Machine shop	Engineering	Total Allocated overhead	Allocated for overhead rate
Department A	$20,000	$ 19,160	$ 3,200	$2,654	$ 4,567	$ 4,716	$ 34,327	171.64%
Department B	40,000	24,080	3,200	1,706	6,896	9,432	45,314	113.29%
Department C	30,000	30,600	9,600	4,171	9,194	7,074	60,639	202.13%
General overhead		20,000	(20,000)	–	–	–		
Storeroom		8,680	800	(9,480)	–	–		
Machine shop		20,360	1,866	759	(22,985)	–		
		17,400	1,334	190	2,298	(21,222)	–	
	$90,000	$140,280	–0–	–0–	–0–	–0–	$140,280	155.87%
			Square footage	Number of requisitions issued	Hours of service	Direct labor of production departments		

Chapter 7

7-1 A cost is allowable (recoverable) as part of indirect cost for government contracts if it is reasonable, properly allocated, not excluded by the procurement regulations, and in accordance with generally accepted accounting principles. The underlying concept is that the government should only reimburse the contractor for those costs necessary to produce the product or provide the service. Those indirect costs not necessary to produce the product or provide the service should not be reimbursed by the government.

7-2   Since all of the work performed by the ZD Corporation was negotiated under the Armed Services Procurement Regulations, I would transfer the bid and proposal cost out of overhead to general and administrative.

Total overhead as presented		$1,256,800
Less: Proposal labor	$175,900	
Proposal new labor	−192,300	−368,200
Adjusted overhead costs		$ 888,600
Direct labor as presented		$1,256,800
Add: Proposal labor		175,900
Adjusted direct labor		$1,432,700
Adjusted overhead rate		62.02%
G&A cost as presented		$ 379,100
Add: Proposal labor	$175,900	
Adjusted overhead at 62.02%	109,093	
Nonlabor proposal costs	192,300	477,293
Adjusted G&A costs		$ 856,393
G&A base		$3,791,000
Less: Cost transferred to G&A		477,293
Adjusted G&A		$3,313,707
Adjusted G&A rate		25.84%

8-1   Since the overhead rate is applied to direct labor and the general and administrative rate is applied to the total of direct labor, overhead, and direct contract charges, the amount of direct contract charges affects the amount of cost recovered. For example, in the rates quoted in the problem, it takes a direct contract charge approximately equal to the direct labor in order for the overhead rate of 73% and a general and administrative rate of 10% to equal a 100% overhead rate on direct labor.

Direct charge	$1.00
Direct labor	1.00
Overhead @ 100%	1.00
Total cost	$3.00
Less: Nonoverhead cost	−2.00
Overhead	$1.00
Direct cost	$1.00
Direct labor	1.00
Overhead @ .73	.73
Overhead cost	$2.73
G & A @ 10%	.27
Total Cost	$3.00
Less: Nonoverhead cost	−2.00
Overhead	$1.00

8-2

Direct labor	$1.00
Fringe @ 28%	.28
	$1.28
Overhead @ 62%	.79
Total cost	$2.07
Less: Direct labor	−1.00
Overhead	$1.07
Direct labor	$1.00
Overhead @ 1.05%	1.05
Total cost	$2.05
Less: Direct labor	1.00
Overhead	$1.05

A fringe rate of 28% and an overhead rate of 62% is higher than a composite rate of 105%.

8-3		
Total overhead		$1,500,000
Total direct labor		$1,500,000
Overhead rate (Total overhead ÷ total direct labor)		100%
Total overhead		$1,500,000
Less: Computer staff overhead		−75,000
Adjusted overhead		$1,425,000
Total direct labor		$1,500,000
Less: Computer staff labor		−125,000
Adjusted direct labor		$1,375,000
Adjusted overhead rate (Adjusted overhead ÷ adjusted direct labor)		103.64%
G&A expense		$ 720,000
G&A base		
Direct labor	$1,500,000	
Overhead	1,500,000	
Direct contract charge	5,000,000	
Total G&A base		$8,000,000
G&A rate (G&A expense ÷ G&A base)		9.0%
G&A expense		$ 720,000
G&A base		
Direct labor	1,375,000	
Overhead	1,425,000	
Direct charge (excludes $1,000,000 of contract computer charges)	4,000,000	
Adjusted G&A base		$6,800,000
G&A rate (G&A expense ÷ adjusted G&A base)		10.59%

8-3 Since the change results in both a higher overhead rate and a higher general and administrative rate, you would not recommend that management make the accounting change.

Worksheets for Calculating Indirect Rates

The first eight exhibits in this appendix represent examples of computation worksheets which outline step-by-step calculation of indirect rates. They are designed to show how the rates are determined using different overhead structures and using variations in the base and grouping of accounts. The assumptions for each exhibit are explained below. Exhibit 9 is a comparison of the rates calculated in the first eight exhibits and illustrates how different overhead structures change the rate even though the same data are used.

The following information is used to calculate the rates for each exhibit.

Labor costs

Direct labor	$350,000
Fringe labor	35,000
Overhead labor	110,000
Selling labor	45,000
G&A labor	60,000
Total labor	$600,000

Nonlabor costs

Direct contract charges	$240,000
Fringe — nonlabor expenses	145,000
Overhead — nonlabor expenses	70,000
Selling — nonlabor expenses	50,000
G&A nonlabor expenses	80,000

Exhibit 1: For this exhibit it is assumed that all fringe benefit costs are included in overhead and the base for calculating the overhead rate is direct production labor. The base for determining the selling expense rate is the sum of the direct production labor and its related overhead and all nonlabor and nonoverhead charges expended on contracts (hereafter referred to direct contract charges). The base for calculating the general and administrative rate is the sum of the selling expense and its base.

Exhibit 2: For Exhibit 2 it is assumed that all fringe benefit costs are again included in overhead and that the base for calculating the overhead rate is direct production labor. The base for determining the selling expense is the sum of the direct production labor, its related overhead and all direct contract charges. The change from Exhibit 1 is that the base for calculating the general and administrative expense rate is the same base that is used for calculating the selling expense rate.

Exhibit 3: Exhibit 3 assumes a separate fringe benefit expense rate. It is calculated by dividing the total fringe benefit expense by the labor costs excluding fringe benefit labor. In others words, the labor that is charged to sick, vacation, or holiday are not included in the denominator. Once this rate has been calculated it is applied to direct labor, overhead labor, selling labor, and general and administrative labor so that the total cost of the expense is distributed over those four labor categories.

The overhead expense is composed of overhead labor, its share of fringe benefit expense and nonlabor overhead expense. The base is the direct labor charged to contracts plus its allocated portion of the fringe benefit expense.

Selling expense is composed of the total selling labor, its distributed share of fringe benefit expense and nonlabor selling ex-

Exhibit 1

(Company Name)	Rate Deviation Worksheet	Period Covered: _____

	L I N E	Total labor (a)	Direct labor (b)	Overhead (c)	Selling (d)	G&A (e)
Total labor (1a − e) (overhead includes fringe benefit labor costs)	1	600,000	350,000	145,000	45,000	60,000
Nonlabor overhead (2c) (overhead includes fringe benefit nonlabor costs)	2			215,000		
Total overhead expense (1c + 2c)	3			360,000		
Overhead rate (3c ÷ 1b)	4			102.86%		
Nonlabor selling expense (5d)	5				50,000	
Total selling expense (1d + 5d)	6				95,000	
Direct contract charges (7a)	7	240,000				
Selling expense base (1b + 3c + 7a)	8				950,000	
Selling expense rate (6d ÷ 8d)	9				10.00%	
Nonlabor G&A expense (10e)	10					80,000
Total G&A expense (1e + 10e)	11					140,000
G&A base (6d + 8d)	12					1,045,000
G&A rate (11e ÷ 12e)	13					13.40%

pense. The base for calculating the selling expense rate is the direct production labor, its related fringe benefit expense, the total overhead expense, and direct contract charges.

Exhibit 2

(Company Name)		Rate Deviation Worksheet				Period Covered: _____

	L I N E	Total labor (a)	Direct labor (b)	Overhead (c)	Selling (d)	G&A (e)
Total labor (1a − e) (overhead includes fringe benefit labor costs)	1	600,000	350,000	145,000	45,000	60,000
Nonlabor overhead (2c) (overhead includes fringe benefit nonlabor costs)	2			215,000		
Total overhead expense (1c + 2c)	3			360,000		
Overhead rate (3c ÷ 1b)	4			102.86%		
Nonlabor selling expense (5d)	5				50,000	
Total selling expense (1d + 5d)	6				95,000	
Direct contract charges (7a)	7	240,000				
Selling expense base (1b + 3c + 7a)	8				950,000	
Selling expense rate (6d ÷ 8d)	9				10.00%	
Nonlabor G&A expense (10e)	10					80,000
Total G&A expense (1e + 10e)	11					140,000
G&A rate (11e ÷ 8d)	12					14.38%

Exhibit 3

(Company Name)   **Rate Deviation Worksheet**   **Period Covered:** _____

	L I N E	Total labor (a)	Direct labor (b)	Overhead (c)	Selling (d)	G&A (e)
Total labor (excluding fringe labor (1a–e)	1	565,000	350,000	110,000	45,000	60,000
Fringe benefit expense (2a) (labor and nonlabor expense)	2	180,000				
Fringe benefit rate (2a ÷ 1a)	3	31.86%				
Fringe benefit distribution 3a x (1a–e)	4	(180,000)	112,000	35,000	14,000	19,000
Nonlabor overhead expense (5c)	5			70,000		
Total overhead expense (1c + 4c + 5c)	6			215,000		
Overhead base (1b + 4b)	7		462,000			
Overhead rate (6c ÷ 7b)	8			46.54%		
Nonlabor selling expense (9d)	9				50,000	
Total selling expense (1d + 4d + 9d)	10				109,000	
Direct contract charges (11a)	11	240,000				
Selling base (6c + 7b + 11a)	12				917,000	
Selling rate (10d ÷ 12d)	13				11.89%	
Nonlabor G&A expense (14e)	14					80,000
Total G&A expense (1e + 4e + 14e)	15					159,000
G&A base (10d + 12d)	16					1,026,000
G&A rate (15e ÷ 16e)	17					15.50%

The total G&A expense is composed of the G&A labor and associated fringe benefit expense, and nonlabor G&A expense. The base for calculating the G&A rate is the selling expense plus its base.

Exhibit 4: This exhibit is calculated the same as Exhibit 3 except the base for calculating the G&A expense rate is the same base that was used for selling expense. In others words, the selling expense is not included in the base for calculating the G&A rate.

Exhibit 5: Exhibit 5 assumes a separate fringe benefit rate. As in Exhibits 3 and 4 the rate is calculated separately and the fringe benefit expense is distributed to four labor categories; Direct Labor, Overhead, Selling, and G&A. The difference is that in this exhibit selling and overhead are combined. The rate is calculated by summarizing the overhead and selling labor, their portions of the fringe benefit expense, and their respective nonlabor expenses and dividing by the total of direct labor and its related fringe benefit expense. The G&A cost is comprised of the labor and associated fringe benefit expense and nonlabor G&A expense, and is divided by the total of direct labor and associated fringe benefit, total overhead expense, and direct contract charges.

Exhibit 6: This exhibit also calculates a separate fringe benefit rate. However, the total fringe benefit expenses (both labor and nonlabor) are divided by the total payroll of the company, which means that labor charged to fringe accounts such as holiday, vacation, and sick leave are included in the denominator. The calculated rate is applied to direct production labor, overhead labor, fringe labor, selling labor and G&A labor. This means that fringe labor shares in the distribution and has some fringe expense allocated to it. This portion of the fringe benefit expense is sometimes referred to as fringe-on-fringe. Because in this assumption all labor shares in the division of the fringe benefit expense, the portion allocated to fringe labor must be reapportioned in order to fully distribute the expense. This distribution to overhead, selling, and G&A expense is based on the amount of labor in those categories. Therefore, the overhead expense is a total of overhead labor, fringe expense, nonlabor overhead expense, and fringe-on-fringe allocation. This is divided by the direct production labor and its share of the fringe benefit expense. To calculate the selling expense rate you summarize selling labor, fringe benefit expense associated with selling labor,

Exhibit 4

(Company Name)	Rate Deviation Worksheet	Period Covered: _____

	LINE	Total labor (a)	Direct labor (b)	Overhead (c)	Selling (d)	G&A (e)
Total labor [excluding fringe labor (1a − e)]	1	565,000	350,000	110,000	45,000	60,000
Fringe benefit expense (2a) (labor and nonlabor expense)	2	180,000				
Fringe benefit rate (2a ÷ 1a)	3	31.86%				
Fringe benefit distribution 3a x (1a − e)	4	180,000	112,000	35,000	14,000	19,000
Nonlabor overhead expense (5c)	5			70,000		
Total overhead expense (1c + 4c + 5c)	6			215,000		
Overhead base (1b + 4b)	7		462,000			
Overhead rate (6c ÷ 7b)	8			46.54%		
Nonlabor selling expense (9d)	9				50,000	
Total selling expense (1d + 4d +9d)	10				109,000	
Direct contract charges (11a)	11	240,000				
Selling and G&A base (6c + 7b + 11a)	12				917,000	
Selling rate (10d ÷ 12d)	13				11.89%	
Nonlabor G&A expense (14e)	14					80,000
Total G&A expense (1e + 4e + 14e)	15					159,000
G&A rate (15e ÷ 12d)	16					17.34%

Exhibit 5

(Company Name)	Rate Deviation Worksheet	Period Covered: _____

	LINE	Total labor (a)	Direct labor (b)	Overhead (c)	Selling (d)	G&A (e)
Total labor [excludes fringe benefit labor (1a − e)]	1	565,000	350,000	110,000	45,000	60,000
Fringe benefit costs (2c) (labor and nonlabor costs)	2	180,000				
Fringe benefit rate (2a ÷ 1a)	3	31.86%				
Fringe benefit distribution 3a x (1a − e)	4	(180,000)	112,000	35,000	14,000	19,000
Nonlabor overhead expense (5c)	5			70,000		
Total overhead expense (1c + 4c + 5c)	6			215,000		
Nonlabor selling expense (7d)	7				50,000	
Total selling expense (1d + 4d + 7d)	8				109,000	
Total overhead expense (6c + 8d)	9			324,000		
Overhead base (1b + 4b)	10		462,000			
Overhead rate (9c ÷ 10b)	11			70.13%		
Nonlabor G&A costs (12e)	12					80,000
Total G&A expense (1e + 4e + 12e)	13					159,000
Direct contract costs (14a)	14	240,000				
G&A base (9c + 100b + 14a)	15					1,026,000
G&A rate (13e ÷ 15e)	16					15.50%

fringe-on-fringe allocation, and nonlabor selling expense. Then divide this by the total of direct production labor including fringe, total overhead expense and direct contract charges. The G&A rate is calculated by taking the G&A expense, its fringe benefit expense allocation, fringe-on-fringe, and non-G&A labor expense, and dividing it by the total of the selling expense and the selling expense base.

Exhibit 7: Exhibit 7 is identical to Exhibit 6 in all calculations except that the base for the G&A rate is the same as the selling expense rate base.

Exhibit 8: Exhibit 8 has separate fringe rate and fringe-on-fringe as Exhibits 6 and 7; however, in this calculation the selling expense has been included as part of overhead. There is no separate selling rate. The G&A expense rate is calculated using a base which includes all direct production labor, its associated fringe, overhead and selling expenses, their related fringe, and direct contract charges.

Exhibit 6

(Company Name)   **Rate Deviation Worksheet**   **Period Covered:** _____

	LINE	Total labor (a)	Direct labor (b)	Overhead (c)	Fringe labor (d)	Selling (e)	G&A (f)
Total labor (1a – f)	1	600,000	350,000	110,000	35,000	45,000	60,000
Fringe benefit cost (2a) (labor and nonlabor expense)	2	180,000					
Fringe benefit rate (2a ÷ 1a)	3	30.00%					
Fringe benefit distribution 3a x(1a – f)	4	(180,000)	105,000	33,000	10,500	13,500	18,000
Nonlabor overhead (5c)	5			70,000			
Fringe-on-fringe distribution 4d ÷ (1c +1e + 1f)	6			5,370	(10,500)	2,200	2,930
Total overhead expense (lc + 4c + 5c + 6c)	7			218,370			
Overhead base (1b + 4b)	8		455,000				
Overhead rate (7c ÷ 8b)	9			47.99%			
Nonlabor selling expense (10e)	10					50,000	
Total selling expense (1e + 4e + 6e + 10e)	11					110,700	
Direct contract charges (12c)	12	240,000					
Selling expense base (7c + 8b + 12a)	13					913,370	
Selling rate (11e ÷ 13e)	14					12.12%	
Nonlabor G&A expense (15f)	15						80,000
Total G&A expense (1f + 4f + 6f + 15f)	16						160,930
G&A base (11e + 13e)	17						1,024,070
G&A rate (16f ÷ 17f)	18						15.71%

Exhibit 7

(Company Name)   **Rate Deviation Worksheet**   Period
                                                                  Covered: _____

	L I N E	Total labor (a)	Direct labor (b)	Overhead (c)	Fringe labor (d)	Selling (e)	G&A (f)
Total labor (1a – f)	1	600,000	350,000	110,000	35,000	45,000	60,000
Fringe benefit cost (2a) (labor and nonlabor expense)	2	180,000					
Fringe benefit rate (2a ÷ 1a)	3	30.00%					
Fringe benefit distribution 3a x (1a – f)	4	(180,000)	105,000	33,000	10,500	13,500	18,000
Nonlabor overhead (5c)	5			70,000			
Fringe-on-fringe distribution 4d ÷ (1c + 1e + 1f)	6			5,370	(10,500)	2,200	2,930
Total overhead expense (1c + 4c + 5c + 6c)	7			218,370			
Overhead base (1b + 4b)	8		455,000				
Overhead rate (7c ÷ 8b)	9			47.99%			
Nonlabor selling expense (10e)	10					50,000	
Total selling expense (1e + 4e + 6e + 10e)	11					110,700	
Direct contract charges (12a)	12	240,000					
Selling and G&A expense rate base (7c + 8b + 12a)	13					913,370	
Selling expense rate (11e ÷ 13e)	14					12.12%	
Nonlabor G&A expense (15f)	15						80,000
Total G&A expense (1f + 4f + 6f + 15f)	16						160,930
G&A rate (16f ÷ 13e)	17						17.62%

Exhibit 8

| (Company Name) | Rate Deviation Worksheet | | | | | Period Covered: _____ |

	LINE	Total labor (a)	Direct labor (b)	Overhead (c)	Fringe labor (d)	Selling (e)	G&A (f)
Total labor (1a–f)	1	600,000	350,000	110,000	35,000	45,000	60,000
Fringe benefit cost (2a) (labor and nonlabor expense)	2	180,000					
Fringe benefit rate (1a ÷ 2a)	3	30.00%					
Fringe benefit distribution 3a x (1a–f)	4	(180,000)	105,000	33,000	10,500	13,500	18,000
Nonlabor overhead (5c)	5			70,000			
Fringe-on-fringe distribution 4d ÷ (1c + 1e + 1f)	6			5,370	(10,500)	2,200	2,930
Total overhead expense (1c + 4c + 5c + 6c)	7			218,370			
Nonlabor selling expense (8e)	8					50,000	
Selling expense (1e + 4e + 6e + 8e)	9					110,700	
Total overhead expense (7c + 9e)	10			329,070			
Overhead base (1b + 4b)	11		455,000				
Overhead rate (10c ÷ 11b)	12			72.32%			
Nonlabor G&A expense (13f)	13						80,000
Total G&A expense (1f + 4f + 6f + 13f)	14						160,930
Direct contract charges (15a)	15	240,000					
G&A base (10c + 11b + 15a)	16						1,024,070
G&A rate (14f ÷ 16f)	17						15.71%

Exhibit 9

Comparison of Indirect Rates
(Exhibits 1 through 8)

	Fringe	Overhead	Selling	G&A
Exhibit 1	—	102.86%	10.00%	13.40%
Exhibit 2	—	102.86%	10.00%	14.38%
Exhibit 3	31.86%	46.54%	11.89%	15.50%
Exhibit 4	31.86%	46.54%	11.89%	17.34%
Exhibit 5	31.86%	70.13%	—	15.50%
Exhibit 6	30.00%	47.99%	12.12%	15.71%
Exhibit 7	30.00%	47.99%	12.12%	17.62%
Exhibit 8	30.00%	72.32%	—	15.71%

APPENDIX C

Allowable and Unallowable Costs for Government Contract Overhead Calculations

I. SPECIFICALLY UNALLOWED COSTS

Listed below are costs that are specifically unallowable. Incurring or charging any of these costs should be avoided. A detailed explanation of the major categories of costs follows. The list of unallowable costs includes:

1. Advertising
   (not help wanted)
2. Bad debt
3. Civil defense donations
4. Contingencies
5. Contributions and donations
6. Entertainment costs
7. Fines and penalties
8. Federal Income Tax
9. Financing costs
10. Incorporation costs and associated costs
11. Interest costs
12. Losses on contracts

The following classifications of expenses represent the most frequently used categories of unallowable costs.

Bad Debts

Bad debts, whether actual or estimated, arising from uncollectable accounts are unallowable. Legal fees and other related collection costs are unallowable when associated with the collection of receivables.

Contingencies

Contingencies are generally set up for some possible future event or condition, which presently is indeterminable. Traditionally, these are unallowable, but they are allowable when they are part of a termination of a contract.

Contributions

The procurement regulations cite contributions and donations as allowable. While the government recognizes the social responsibilities of companies, they contend that, if contributions were allowable, then, in fact, the government is the one that is making the contribution and not the contractor. Be sure to classify your costs correctly because payments to professional societies, if classified correctly, are allowable costs and are not to be considered contributions.

Entertainment Costs

Entertainment costs, including the costs of amusement and social activities and incidental costs such as those related to meals, lodging, and gratuities, are generally unallowable.

Fines and Penalties

The cost of fines and penalties resulting from violation or failure of the contractor to comply with federal, state, and local laws is unallowable.

Interest and Interest Costs

Interest and borrowings are not allowable regardless of how they are cast. Any professional fees and legal fees paid in connection with preparation of a prospectus or preparation and issuance of stock rights are unallowable.

Losses on Contracts

Any excess cost over income on contracts cannot be considered an allowable cost in overhead.

Organizational Cost

Expenditures that are necessary to incorporate the business, including incorporation fees, attorneys' fees, accountants' fees, and brokers' fees, are not allowable. Also, fees and costs related to organization and reorganization of business for raising capital are not allowable costs.

II. ALLOWABLE COSTS – SELECTED SAMPLES

The following classification of expenses represent the most frequently used categories of allowable costs.

Advertising Costs

Advertising cost that include those costs incurred solely for the recruitment of personnel required by the contractor for performance of obligations arising under contracts are allowable. This covers the cost of advertising in media such as magazines, newspapers, television, radio, direct mail, trade papers, outdoor advertising, conventions, exhibits, free goods, and samples.

Bidding Costs

Bidding costs include the cost of preparing proposals on potential government contracts, including the engineering, scientific, manufacturing, and cost data necessary to support the contractor's proposal. It includes both the cost of successful and unsuccessful bids prepared in the current accounting period. Bidding costs incurred in past accounting fiscal years will never be considered allowable in the current fiscal year. All elements of expense can be charged to this expense category (i.e., labor, travel, supplies, computer, printing, etc.).

Bonding Costs

Bonding costs occur when the contractor is required to get assurance against financial loss in case of default or failure to complete the contract. All bonding costs required pursuant to the terms of the contract are allowable. Also allowable are those costs that would be considered of a general nature required in business as long as sound business practices are followed and the rates are reasonable under the circumstances.

Civil Defense Cost

Civil defense costs are those incurred for planning and for protection against possible enemy attacks. These costs are considered allowable. If the cost is of such significant amount that it can be considered an asset, then the depreciation costs are allowable. However, contributions to local and civil defense funds and projects are unallowable.

Compensation for Personnel Services

This substantial category of costs is broken into several parts, which include salary and wages, cash bonuses, incentive compensation, stock options, deferred compensation, and fringe benefits. Overall, the procurement regulations have indicated that, as long as the amount is reasonable and generally conforms to compensation paid by other firms of the same size in the same industry, or in the same geographical area for similar service, then they are an allowable cost. The auditors generally lump all these costs together to see if the overall compensation is reasonable, even though the costs may be charged in different categories in the accounting system. The auditors are particularly interested in any changes in salary levels that concur with an increase in the ratio of government contracts to other business, or any change in the treatment of allowability of specific types of compensation due to having increased government work.

Wages and Salaries. This includes the gross compensation paid to employees in the form of cash, products, or services and are allowable costs.

Cash Bonuses and Incentive Compensation. Cash bonuses and incentive compensation include incentive compensation for management employees, cash bonuses, suggestion awards, safety awards, and incentive compensation based on production, cost reduction, and efficient performances. These are allowable when the overall compensation is determined to be reasonable and is paid or accrued according to an agreement entered into in good faith between the contractors and their employees before the services are rendered, or according to an established plan followed so consistently by the contractor that it has become an implied agreement between the employer and employee.

Deferred Compensation. Deferred compensation includes all remunerations, in no matter what form, that the employee has earned but is not paid until after a stated period of time has elapsed or some events have occurred, as provided in a plan. These costs include contributions, pensions, annuities, stock bonuses, and profit-sharing plans and are allowable.

Fringe Benefits. Fringe benefits are allowances and services provided by the contractor to his employees as compensation in addition to regular salary or wages, including such things as vacation, holidays, sick leave, military leave, employee insurance, unemployment benefit plans, severance pay, training, and education.

Depreciation

Depreciation represents the charge to current operation that distributes the cost of the tangible capital asset over the useful life of an asset in some systematic or logical manner. It is considered an allowable cost.

Economic Development Costs

This group of costs includes the cost of generalized long-range management planning concerned with the future overall development of the firm's business.

Employee Morale, Health, and Welfare

Employee morale, health and welfare activities are those services or benefits provided by the contractor for the employees to improve working conditions or employee-employer relations and employee performance. Such activities include house publications, first-aid clinics, recreation, and food and dormitory services. The food and dormitory services, including operating or furnishing facilities such as cafeterias or dining rooms, are allowable. However, any income received from these must be credited to the account so that only net cost is the portion that is allowable.

Losses on food operation may be included in cost only if it is the contractor's objective to operate such services on a break-even basis.

Excess Facilities Cost

The cost of having and maintaining housing in excess of contractor-owned facilities is unallowable. In other words, if there is more space than needed for any length of time, the government may not allow the cost.

Insurance

Insurance that the contractor is required to carry or insurance that he must maintain in connection with the general conduct of his business is allowable, provided the premiums and rates are considered reasonable. When a contractor provides for self-insurance under an approved program, the costs are allowable to the extent that the same type of coverage and rates and premiums would be allowed if it were purchased outside to cover the cost of risks.

Labor Relations Costs

Costs of maintaining satisfactory labor relations between the contractor and employees, including shop stewards, labor management committees, and employee publications, are allowable.

Maintenance and Repair Costs

Costs necessary for the upkeep of the property (including government property) that neither add to the permanent value nor appreciably extend its useful life, but whose primary purpose is to keep the equipment in efficient operating condition, are allowable.

Other Business Expenses

The category of other business expenses includes such reoccurring expenses as registry and transfer charges resulting from change in ownership of securities, cost of shareholders' meetings, normal proxy solicitation, preparation of shareholder report publications, preparation and submission of required reports and forms to taxing and other regulatory bodies, and incidental costs of directors' and committee meetings. These are allowed costs when allocated on an equitable basis to the government work.

Patent Cost

Costs of preparing disclosures, reports, and other documents in filing of patent applications where the title is conveyed to the government are allowable.

Plant Protection Cost

Plant protection costs — items such as wages, uniforms, equipment for personnel engaged in plant security, and any depreciational plant protection capital equipment — are allowable.

Pre-contract Cost

Pre-contract costs are those costs incurred prior to the effective date of the contract that are related to a negotiation and are a necessary cost in anticipation of the award of the contract in order for the contractor to comply with the proposed contract delivery schedule. Such costs are allowable in overhead to the extent that they would have been allowed under the contract had they been incurred after the date of the contract.

Professional Services — Legal, Accounting, Engineering, and Other

Costs of professional services rendered by members of a particular profession who are not employees of the contract are allowable, provided they are incurred in the conduct of the general business of the corporation.

Recruitment Costs

Recruitment costs, which include the cost of help wanted advertising, fees paid to commercial agencies, cost of operating the employment or personnel office, and travel cost of applicants for interviews, are considered allowable costs.

Relocation Cost

Relocation costs are costs incurred for a permanent change of duty assignment, usually defined as an infinite period or a stated period of no less than 12 months for a current employee or upon the recruitment of a new employee. This includes, but is not limited to, the transportation to the new location of the employee, members of his immediate family, and his household and personal effects, the cost of temporary living quarters, advance trips by employee and spouse to locate new living quarters, and some other necessary, reasonable expenses normally incidental to relocation.

Rental Costs

Rental costs of land, building, equipment, and other personal property are allowable if the rates are reasonable in light of rental costs of comparable facilities and market conditions in the area. The auditor will generally look at the amount of rental, particularly in the area of leases. They recognize that in the lease cost are interest and profit to the company leasing the equipment. Generally, leasing is a question of degree with an auditor. If it is a small amount, he will generally not question it. If a large portion of the equipment is rented or leased, it may be questioned and only the cost you would be able to depreciate if you owned it would be allowable.

Selling Cost

Selling costs arise in the marketing of the contractor's products or services and include sales, promotion, and negotiation. They are allowable to the extent that they are reasonable and allocable to government business.

Severance Pay

Severance pay, also called dismissal wages, is payment in addition to regular salary and wages by the contractor to workers whose employment has been terminated. Costs of severance pay are allowable only to the extent that is required by law or through an employer-employee agreement or an established policy that, in effect, implies an agreement.

Taxes

Taxes charged by the federal government, such as income taxes, are not allowable. State taxes and sales taxes are allowable costs in overhead. However, any penalties and fines related to these are not allowable.

Trade, Business, Technical and Professional Activity Costs

Trade, business, technical, and professional activity costs included in this category are the following:

Meetings and conferences. This item includes cost of meals, transportation, rental facilities for meetings, and other related costs when the primary purpose of such a meeting is a dissemination of technical information. Such costs are allowable, but these types of costs are subject to the policy of the corporation concerning payment of this type of expense.

Memberships. This includes the cost of memberships in trade, business, or technical and professional organizations and are allowable.

Subscriptions. This includes the cost of subscriptions to trade, business, or technical periodicals and are allowable.

Training and Education Costs

Training and education costs, the costs of preparation and maintenance of a program of instruction for employees to improve efficiency, are allowable. It includes, but is not limited to, on-the-job, classroom, and apprenticeship training, and includes all the costs to the employee, including materials and textbooks.

Transportation Cost

Transportation costs include the freight, cartage, and postage charges relating either to goods, purchases, or services delivered. The costs are allowable. Where such costs can be readily identified, they should be charged directly to contracts.

Travel Cost

Travel cost includes the cost of transportation, lodging, subsistence, and incidental costs incurred by the contractor's personnel while in travel on official company business. They may be paid upon actual cost incurred, or on a per diem or mileage basis in lieu of actual costs; a combination of the two can also be used. Travel costs are allowable, and this is one of the classes of cost that is generally both direct and indirect. The costs of air travel by coach or economy class are allowable. The cost of travel by first class in not allowable unless the first-class accommodations must be taken in order to meet required deadlines.

Definition of Expense Classification

The following definition of accounts is divided into two parts — expenses by type and expenses by purpose. They are presented to familiarize the reader with the flexibility and the options available in establishing the definitions. The list of accounts is not intended to cover all accounts but to be fully representative of the usual practice and definition.

Expense by Type (Part 1) — These accounts are representative of the classification used by the management who want to know accumulated costs according to the source or nature of the expense. It is the purest system for recording the costs because all costs within the classification generally are generated from the same source. For example, if management wanted to know the telephone costs of the organization, it would establish an account called "telephone" and all costs related to telephone, including rental, line usage, message unit costs, and advertising in the yellow pages page costs, would be accumulated in that one account. It is possible to have a telephone account in each of the operating units so management could know the cost of telephone for each unit. But it would not provide information as to why the telephone was being used. That is, to make sales, cost, to perform services directly related to contracts, or to carry on the general business of the organization.

Expense by Purpose (Part 2) — In order to allow management to collect information on why the expense is being incurred, the classification expense by purpose is established. The accounts designated in Part 2 of Appendix D are representative of accounts used by management who are more interested in why the expense was incurred and may only be secondarily interested in the nature or the source of the expense. The expenses in this classification are not all of one type but are an accumulation of different types of expenses grouped according to the reason for incurring the expense.

PART I – EXPENSES BY TYPE

Indirect Labor

Executive. The executive account will cover all compensation paid to officers when performing work of a general corporate nature, and which is associated with the corporate general (executive) section.

Supervisory. The supervisory account will cover all compensation paid to supervisory employees whose main function is to direct the work of others. This account will be charged by managers when directing the work of employees in their own departments.

Administrative and Clerical. The administrative and clerical account will cover compensation to employees who are not directly chargeable to a specific project. All secretarial work, departmental assistance, etc., will be charged to this account.

Proposal Preparation. The proposal preparation account will cover compensation paid to employees for estimating effort and proposal preparation.

General Engineering. In the general engineering account will be recorded compensation to engineers and draftsmen for that time worked that was not chargeable to a specific project.

Repair and Maintenance — Building

The building repair and maintenance account will cover the compensation paid to plant personnel in connection with the repair and maintenance of buildings. This account is for labor charges only. Materials incidental to repairs and maintenance will be charged to a different repair and maintenance account.

NOTE: When repair and maintenance services are performed by other than plant personnel, the charge will be to the expense account, Outside Services — Repair and Maintenance, Building.

Repair and Maintenance — Machinery and Equipment

Included in the machinery and equipment repair and maintenance account are the labor charges incidental to repair and maintenance of machinery, test equipment, office furniture, fixtures, and transportation equipment.

NOTE: When repair and maintenance services are performed by other than plant personnel the charge will be the expense account, Outside Services — Repair and Maintenance, Equipment.

Moving and Rearranging

This includes the moving and rearranging of office furniture and fixtures, machinery, and equipment, when such services are performed by company personnel.

Janitorial

Included in the janitorial account is the compensation paid for janitors.

Operating Services

The operating services account includes compensation to storekeepers, stock clerks, shipping and receiving, warehousemen, inventory taking, etc.

Conferences, Technical Papers, and Lectures

The conferences, technical papers, and lectures account covers compensation paid to employees for time spent at conferences, technical discussions, conventions and symposia, writing a technical paper, or delivering a lecture.

Accounting Services

The accounting services account will cover compensation paid the administrative staff in performing accounting functions.

Personnel Services

The personnel services account will cover all compensation paid the administrative staff in performing personnel services.

Contracts Services

The contracts services account covers compensation paid to the administrative staff in performing contracts services.

Administrative Services

Compensation for administrative services, including those of the manager, the receptionist, and the mail room clerk, are recorded in the administrative services account.

Idle and Allowed Time Accounts

Allowed Time. Included in the allowed time account is all compensation paid to direct labor employees for time lost due to lack of material, set-up, inspection, and mechanical and electrical failures, etc.

Training and Instruction. Payment to instructors and/or trainees for hours of actual instruction and training during which no production is accomplished is covered in the training and instruction account.

Personal Business. The personal business account is charged with compensation paid to employees for a period of absence for the purpose of attending to personal business. (Prior approval of supervisor is necessary.)

First Aid. First aid compensation is paid to employees for periods of absence for the purpose of receiving first aid treatment.

Labor Additives/Surcharges Accounts

Payroll Taxes. The payroll taxes account will include only those payroll taxes applicable to the current period that are due and payable by the company as an employer. These costs represent only the employer's share.

Unemployment Payroll Taxes. All unemployment payroll taxes, both federal and state, due and payable by the company as an employer, are included in the unemployment payroll taxes account.

Group Insurance. The group insurance account will cover the cost for the current period of the company-sponsored group insurance program.

Workers' Compensation. Included in the workers' compensation account as expense are all payments made by the company in connection with industrial injury cases arising from injuries or sickness that are covered by workers' compensation laws.

Vacation (for accounting use only – not for time reporting). The vacation account includes the pro rata accrual, applicable to the current period, of the estimated annual vacation expense. DO NOT CHARGE this account with compensation paid employees at time of vacation.

Holiday (for accounting use only – not for time reporting). Include in this holiday account the pro rata accrual, applicable to the current period, of the estimated annual holiday expense. DO NOT CHARGE this account with compensation paid employees at time of holiday.

Sick Leave — for time reporting. Include in this sick leave account time applicable to sick leave compensation paid employees for time off for being ill.

Profit-Sharing Expense. This profit-sharing account will be charged for the company contribution to the employees' profit-sharing trust.

Supplies and Indirect Materials Accounts

Repairs and Maintenance Material. Costs of materials used in connection with the repairs and maintenance of office furniture and fixtures, machinery and equipment, and transportation equipment make up one account.

Operating Supplies. Operating supplies include the cost of materials purchased for normal and routine operating purposes that are not chargeable to a specific product or project. Operating supplies include oils, greases, gasoline, and other items that must be maintained.

Other Supplies. Other supplies of an indirect nature that are not correctly chargeable to any other account make up a separate account. Example: first aid and safety supplies.

Professional and Outside Services Accounts

Professional Services — Accounting and Auditing. Costs of technical or professional services rendered by outside agents make up a separate personal services account.

Outside Services — Repair and Maintenance, Building and Equipment. An outside services account will be charged with the cost of repair and maintenance to building and equipment by outside vendors.

Outside Services − Moving and Rearranging. The cost of moving and rearranging performed by other than company employees is accounted for in an outside services category.

Outside Services − Other. Other outside services are placed in a separate account where the costs of any outside services not covered elsewhere are recorded.

Outside Service − Computer. An outside service computer account covers the cost of outside computer services.

Utilities and Transportation Accounts

Power, Heat, Fuel, and Water. The power, heat, fuel, and water account will be used to record the amount paid or accrued for current period power, light, heat, and water expense.

Telephone, Telegraph, and Teletype. This telephone, telegraph, and teletype account will be used to record the cost of telephone, telegraph, and teletype services.

Postage. Included in the postage account are the costs of stamps, parcel post, postage meter rental and consumption, registered letter fees, and all items of a postage nature.

Freight and Cartage. The freight and cartage account will cover both incoming and outgoing freight, express, cartage, and similar charges not applicable to a specific project or fixed asset.

Truck and Auto. Charge to this truck and auto account with expenses of company-owned or leased vehicles. This account DOES NOT cover drivers' salaries or wages.

Advertising, Publicity, and Promotions Accounts

Advertising. The advertising account is charged with the costs of newspaper, trade papers, periodicals, or other media advertisements.

Promotional Material. Expenses incurred in connection with publications reprints, photographic reprints and other items of a promotional material nature are charged to the promotional material account.

Conventions and Exhibits. The conventions and exhibits account will include expenses incurred for floor space and construction of booths and displays and other expenses of conventions and exhibits for presentation of company products.

Advertising – Other. An Advertising – Other account will cover expenses of a publicity, advertising, and promotional nature not applicable to other advertising classifications.

Travel, Luncheons, and Entertainment Accounts

Travel. This travel account will include all costs incurred by employees while traveling on company business. It includes transportation costs, hotel or motel accommodations, meals, automobile mileages, allowance for travel by personal automobile, and similar items of traveling expense as authorized by company policy. (Persons traveling on company business for a particular project or product will charge their time to that project or product.)

Luncheons and Dinners. Cost of business luncheons and dinners for employees, customers, etc. in attendance at professional and business meetings where the registration fee will be considered part of the same cost is charged to a luncheons and dinners account.

Entertainment. Costs incurred in connection with the entertainment of customers for the purpose of promoting business relations is charged to the entertainment account. It will include the cost of hotel accommodations, dinners, amusement, etc., for employees and those being entertained.
NOTE: DO NOT INCLUDE any items of expense that are properly chargeable to traveling, or to luncheons and dinners accounts.

Conferences. The conferences account will include cost of fees paid for conference attendance and related expenses but will exclude the cost of time and travel expenses.

Employment, Recruitment, and Employee Welfare Accounts

Interviews and Employment Expense (Recruitee Only). Expenses other than travel incurred in connection with interviewing potential employees is charged to the interviews and employment expense account (for recruitee only).

Help Wanted Advertising. Included in the help wanted advertising account are expenses of placing ads in newspapers and trade papers, and any other help wanted advertisements.

Relocation Expense. The relocation expense account includes expenses incidental to the transfer or relocation of employees.

Occupancy Expenses Accounts

Taxes — State. A state tax expense account is used to record state income taxes.

Taxes — Property. A property taxes account will record property tax expense.

General Insurance. A general insurance account will record general insurance coverage.

Rent — Building. The rental expense of buildings is covered in the rent — building account.

Depreciation. The depreciation expense on company-owned property is charged to the depreciation account.

Amortization. Charge the amortization account with the amortization of leasehold improvements.

Rent – Equipment. This rent – equipment account will include the rental expense of equipment.

Sundry Group Accounts

Membership Dues. A membership dues account is charged with the cost of membership dues in trade, technical, or other associations.

Subscriptions. Subscription costs of daily newspapers, periodicals, magazines, technical bulletins, etc. are part of the subscriptions account.

Donations and Contributions. All properly authorized donations made by the company to various charitable organizations are charged to donations and contributions accounts.

Sundry. The sundry account is used to record expenses that do not properly fit elsewhere in the expense classifications.

PART II – EXPENSES BY PURPOSES

Bid and Proposal Costs – Description

Charge all costs of preparing proposals to this bid and proposal cost account. All costs of preparing the proposal, such as time sheet charges, printing and reproduction, travel, and subsequent contract negotiations, shall be charged.

This account would also include time and expenses incurred in discussing general proposal and promotion, correspondence and meetings of a general nature with clients, and other miscellaneous proposal and promotional costs. Expenses to be included are local transportation costs (cabs, mileage, parking fees, car rentals, hotels, meals, baggage, and handling).

Personnel Placement

The personnel placement account is charged with all costs related to the recruitment or placement of personnel, help wanted ads, fees paid to employment agencies in search and ultimate placement of qualified personnel, relocation expenses paid new personnel to relocate them to the place of original employment, and expenses such as travel and other related costs for college and university recruitment. Also in this account, include luncheons or dinners with prospective staff members. Also include moving expenses that result from relocation where the relocation is not occasioned by work requirements chargeable to a specific contract.

Specific Professional Development Activities

The specific professional development activities account accumulates all labor costs associated with the professional development courses established by management. Costs include course registrations, time sheet charges while attending course, travel costs, hotel, meals, and any special purchases, if required, of attendee. For company-initiated courses, include time charges for preparation, typing, printing and reproduction, equipment rental, and other supplies. If the company-initiated course is conducted away from the office, include cost for conference room rental, travel costs, room and meals, equipment rental (used in conference), etc.

Internal Communications

Charge the internal communications account with the preparation, typing and reproduction of the secretaries' manual, accounting manual, chart of accounts, profit-sharing booklets, wage and salary manual, employee handbook, and project managers' manual. Charge this account for all time spent in preparing for and attending management committee meetings, profit-sharing meetings, and monthly staff meetings.

Office Supplies and General Office Account

The office supplies account includes the cost of all office services. It includes items necessary for basic office activity of the operating departments, such as, but not limited to, general stationery supplies, small furniture and fixture items (under $100 not capitalized), typewriter supplies, and basic working materials, such as pens, pencils, working pads, file folders, ledgers, books and periodicals, graph paper, drawing supplies, and tools.

The Accounting Equation

The basic accounting equation is:
Assets = Liabilities + Equity

This equation has all the properties and rights of an algebraic equation. Any arithmetic operation can be done to both sides of the equation without changing its value. For instance, liabilities can be subtracted from both sides of the equation so that your equation would read: **assets – liabilities = equity.** However, before a discussion of how the equation works, a brief definition of the terms is appropriate.

Assets. Assets can be divided into two groups — current assets and fixed assets. Assets are something of value (whether tangible or intangible), which are owned and used to generate income.

Current Assets. The current asset classifications are items that are readily converted into cash. These include such items as cash, accounts receivable, or inventories that will be converted to cash through sales in the near future or can be easily converted to cash through a forced sale.

Fixed Assets. Fixed assets are those items that are kept in the business for a long time. They are generally more permanent in nature and, as a rule, are written off over long periods of time, except in the case of land, which is never depreciated. They are generally not easily converted into cash and retain their value as assets to the corporation because they have a useful life over the long-term operation of the business.

Liabilities. Liabilities are debts that are owed for products or services that include both present and future liabilities. Like assets, they are grouped according to the currentness of the liability.

Current Liabilities. Current liabilities are those that are due to be paid in less than one year. They include the portion of the long-term liability that is due for payment within the year. For example, if a note due at the bank for $45,000 is payable in three (3) installments of $15,000 per year, the first year's $15,000 would be a current liability.

Long-Term Liabilities. Long-term liabilities are those that are payable after one year. In the example stated above, the balance of $30,000 of the $45,000 note would be a long-term liability.

Equity. Equity is the proprietorship. it's the excess of assets over liabilities and is what the owner owns. It is also the right of ownership of assets and responsibility for liabilities.

This section is broken down into the capital that has been contributed by the individuals, the earnings from prior years that have been retained by the firm, and the results of the current year's operation. This means the equity section of the equation can be further broken down as follows:

Equity = Stock Ownership + Retained Earnings from Prior Year + Earnings from Current Year.

The current year's earnings can be further segregated: Income − Expenses. The expanded accounting equation would now read:

Assets = Liabilities + (Stock Ownership + Retained Earnings from Prior Year + Income − Expenses)

The income less the expense represents the results of operations during the year. These accounts are summarized into what is known as a profit and loss statement or a Statement of Operations.

The assets, liabilities, and equity accounts (this includes the stock ownership, the retained earnings, and the results of the current operations) represent the accounts that are included in the balance sheet or Statement of Financial Position. This statement reflects the financial condition of the company at a point in time.

Each member of the equation is a collection of individual records or accounts representing similar items. The balance in the account is affected by entries made to the account from the summary of business transactions that take place during the accounting period. These entries would come from several sources, such as cash receipts, cash disbursements, payroll, etc. These entries, while taking many forms and coming from many source documents, are beyond the scope of this appendix. However, there is always one element that is consistent — the sum of all of the debit entries will equal the sum of the credit entries. Keep in mind that a debit entry means an entry on the left side of the account and a credit means an entry on the right side of the account.

The old story about debits being those near the window and credits being those near the door is more truth than fiction. Debit does not stand for debtor and credit does not stand for creditor. These terms literally have come to mean left and right, respectively.

So, if each grouping of the accounting equation were visualized as representative of what is known as a T account (where the left side represented debits and the right side represented credits), then it becomes clear how debits and credits affect this balance in the account:

Assets			Liabilities			Equity		
Debit	Credit	=	Debit	Credit	+	Debit	Credit	+
(+)	(−)		(−)	(+)		(−)	(+)	

	Income			Expenses	
	Debit	Credit	−	Debit	Credit
	(−)	(+)		(+)	(−)

Increases or decreases to the accounting equation can be summarized as follows:

Debits indicate:
>> asset increases
>> liability decreases
>> equity decreases
>> income decreases
>> expenses increases

Credits indicate just the opposite:
>> asset decreases
>> liability increases
>> equity increases
>> income increases
>> expenses decreases

In terms of balance sheet equations, there are only nine fundamental types of transactions. They are as follows:

Asset increases accompanied by:
>> asset decreases
>> liability increases
>> equity increases

Liability decreases accompanied by:
>> asset decreases
>> liability increases
>> equity increases

Equity decreases accompanied by:
>> asset decreases
>> liability increases
>> equity increases

This brief review of the accounting equation is not intended to fully train the person completely unfamiliar with accounting principles, but will provide a framework for understanding the effects of all entries in the accounting equation.

Index